LIBRARY MANUALS

Volume 8

LIBRARY LOCAL COLLECTIONS

LIBRARY LOCAL COLLECTIONS

W.C. BERWICK SAYERS

LONDON AND NEW YORK

First published 1939 by George Allen & Unwin Ltd
This edition first published in 2022
by Routledge
4 Park Square, Milton Park, Abingdon, Oxon OX14 4RN
and by Routledge
605 Third Avenue, New York, NY 10017
Routledge is an imprint of the Taylor & Francis Group, an informa business

Copyright © 1939 by Taylor & Francis.

All rights reserved. No part of this book may be reprinted or reproduced or utilised in any form or by any electronic, mechanical, or other means, now known or hereafter invented, including photocopying and recording, or in any information storage or retrieval system, without permission in writing from the publishers.

Trademark notice: Product or corporate names may be trademarks or registered trademarks, and are used only for identification and explanation without intent to infringe.

British Library Cataloguing in Publication Data
A catalogue record for this book is available from the British Library

ISBN: 978-1-03-213109-2 (Set)
ISBN: 978-1-00-322771-7 (Set) (ebk)
ISBN: 978-1-03-213366-9 (Volume 8) (hbk)
ISBN: 978-1-03-213369-0 (Volume 8) (pbk)
ISBN: 978-1-00-322888-2 (Volume 8) (ebk)

DOI: 10.4324/9781003228882

Publisher's Note
The publisher has gone to great lengths to ensure the quality of this reprint but points out that some imperfections in the original copies may be apparent.

Disclaimer
The publisher has made every effort to trace copyright holders and would welcome correspondence from those they have been unable to trace.

LIBRARY LOCAL COLLECTIONS

by

W. C. BERWICK SAYERS

CHIEF LIBRARIAN OF
CROYDON, PRESIDENT
OF THE LIBRARY
ASSOCIATION
1938

LONDON
GEORGE ALLEN & UNWIN LTD
MUSEUM STREET

FIRST PUBLISHED IN 1939

All rights reserved
PRINTED IN GREAT BRITAIN BY
UNWIN BROTHERS LTD., WOKING

GENERAL INTRODUCTION TO THE SERIES

by W. E. DOUBLEDAY, HON. F.L.A.

THIS new Series of Handbooks is intended to supplement the larger Manuals issued by Messrs. George Allen & Unwin and the Library Association under the title of *The Library Association Series of Library Manuals*.

There are some aspects of Library Work which, although by no means unimportant, are of themselves insufficient to require a full-sized manual, and there are other phases which in a comprehensive textbook of manageable dimensions could be dealt with only in a general way. The Handbooks will adequately cover these subjects and will also treat of certain special topics which hitherto have escaped the attention which they deserve, or which—owing to recent developments—demand reconsideration.

Since Library practice must always be in accordance with the particular requirements of different types and sizes of Libraries, variant methods will be indicated from time to time, and a working basis for individual adoption and comparative study will thus be provided. University, Municipal, School, and Special Libraries—rural as well as urban—will be comprehended within the scope of the Practical Library Handbooks, and in each instance the latest advances will be described.

LIBRARY LOCAL COLLECTIONS

This smaller Series is issued independently by Messrs. George Allen & Unwin Ltd., and the range is sufficiently wide to make the volumes appeal to Administrators, Librarians, Assistants, and Students who intend to sit at the professional examinations. It is hoped that they will be of great practical assistance for immediate use in enhancing and forwarding still further that improvement in Library service which has been so marked since the passing of the Public Libraries Act of 1919.

PREFACE

> That which thy father olde
> Hath left thee to possesse:
> Doe thou that dearlie holde
> To show hys worthynesse.
>
> —*Old Inscription used as the motto of the Photographic Record and Survey of Surrey.*

THIS little book on one of my enthusiasms has been written in the busiest year of my life, and must have many shortcomings. It claims to be no more than a brief description of work which I have seen done with some success in the collecting, conserving, and exploiting of the materials of local history. Much of this I naturally learned at my own library, especially when I was working with Mr. L. Stanley Jast. It follows that Croydon and its Surrey collection figure largely in my pages, and I ask other librarians who are doing this work elsewhere to forgive that in the hope that something may emerge from it which may interest them.

I do not possess any special knowledge of many things which form part of a good local collection, and this will be quite obvious to the expert who may glance through it. My concern has been with the obvious interest of the work, and with methods of handling material rather than with an exposition of what is to be found in that material. The list of books at the end, which I owe to Dr. C. B. M. Sillick, contains as much as any librarian, who is interested to pursue subjects further, is likely to absorb, unless his aim is to become a specialist.

I am indebted to the various authorities whom I have quoted, as, quite clearly, a book like this must be mainly the work of others. To my colleagues, Mr. Henry A. Sharp, Mr. Kenneth Ryde, and Miss Alicia J. Culverwell, I have to make acknowledgments for assistance.

W. C. BERWICK SAYERS

CONTENTS

GENERAL INTRODUCTION TO THE SERIES	7
PREFACE	9
I. OUR PURPOSE	15
II. WHAT IS COLLECTED	24
III. THE COST AND METHODS OF COLLECTION	31
IV. ARRANGEMENT AND CATALOGUING	48
V. DEEDS AND MANUSCRIPTS	64
VI. GRAPHIC RECORDS: PAINTINGS, PRINTS, AND DRAWINGS	73
VII. PHOTOGRAPHIC AND REGIONAL SURVEY RECORDS	79
VIII. MAPS AND PLANS	92
IX. THE HOUSING AND FILING OF THE COLLECTION	97
X. MISCELLANEOUS. LIBRARIES OF MUNICIPAL REFERENCE. COPIES. EXPLOITING THE COLLECTION. NOTABLE CATALOGUES. CONCLUSION	104
APPENDIX	
USEFUL BOOKS AND ARTICLES	111
INDEX	125

THE SHAKESPEARE LIBRARY IN THE BIRMINGHAM PUBLIC REFERENCE LIBRARY

[Courtesy of the Chief Librarian, and the Oxford University Press]

ILLUSTRATIONS

FACING PAGE

THE SHAKESPEARE LIBRARY IN THE BIRMINGHAM PUBLIC REFERENCE LIBRARY *Frontispiece*

THE EDINBURGH ROOM IN THE EDINBURGH CENTRAL PUBLIC LIBRARY 22

MEMBER'S CARD, THE PHOTOGRAPHIC SURVEY AND RECORD OF SURREY 80

THE SUSSEX ROOM IN THE WORTHING CENTRAL PUBLIC LIBRARY 96

LIBRARY LOCAL COLLECTIONS

CHAPTER I

OUR PURPOSE

ALL roads and paths in the English village centre in the church; from there has radiated much of English life, its ethics, laws, ways of speech; such art as it knew was in its architecture, its frescoes, painted roofs, and stained glass; and its monuments linked the generations. In short, it was, and is, the brief abstract and chronicle of the life of our people. This is merely one objective statement of a fact to be discerned by all who care to contemplate our country for a few minutes from the point of view of its story. Such villages are only a microcosm of the whole. The imaginative man of to-day, passing along an English road, if he have time to observe it well, must see that thousands of years of human life lie behind so contracted an area as the British Isles. The windings of the roads on which he moves, the contours of the hills, courses of streams, shapes of fields and woodlands with the apparently erratic directions of hedges and banks, the colour of the soil—white, red, brown, black—the siting of church and homestead; all these are what they are because Nature and Man move in relationship, and

Man has accepted his necessities. In the British Isles there can be few corners which are not in their measure shrines of the long interesting past of our country:

> All that tread
> The globe are but a handful to the tribes
> That slumber in its bosom.

Ignorance of these things is natural enough, but the map lives only if we are aware of its history. It is a familiar paradox that many men can recount some part of the history of Rome, or even of Polynesia, who are without the most vague idea of the history of the street in which they dwell. Some, in and near London, do not even know under what local authority they live. Yet, by another paradox, when local history is brought before them in any living way they are alert enough to read or hear. The recognition of this in this century has brought educators to the view that the best approach to history in general is through the history of the home town or village; that the best subject which a child may use is one of his own neighbourhood, and that national life and government from their origins to well on into our complex modern forms of them can be studied on the spot where pupil and teacher are standing. The newly-built town or suburb has this racial history as well as the old town, if in a lesser degree.

The interest and importance of this study may be brought out if one makes a collection of facts on the place-names in one's own town. To narrow it down to the streets; how did they come to be named as they are? Obvious reasons present themselves for the various "Church" streets, lanes, and alleys, although it will sometimes be found that subsequently interposed buildings make the names seem to be misplaced. That they do seem to, leads us to discover why, and so a new set of facts emerges. "High" streets are usually simply explained. Then, a study of old maps, enclosure awards, and similar documents, shows that a great many names are survivals of landowners who have long faded from memory. A whole series will be found to indicate when roads were built, as do those of Alma and Inkermann from Crimea time, and Consuelo and Tugela from the Boer War; there are many such. Again, prominent citizens, mayors, council-members, and so on, have often their most lasting memorial in street names. Some notion, too, of the literary, artistic, and other propensities of the people may be inferred from streets which bear the names of poet, artist, and musician. Some tell us where their builder was born or spent his honeymoon, and the names of his children. The method may be extended to open spaces and public buildings, and, perhaps most of all, to private homes. A whole world of information is obtained in this way, the results of which are remarkably illuminating as well as useful. Towns, the most commonplace superficially, are nearly always vivid with romance. It must not be inferred from this that I expect the local collector to be the local historian as a matter of course. He is, in fact, often so, but the main purpose of the collector is to get the material together from which any other worker may make the deductions of the historian. I do mean that if some systematic approach, of which the study of street names is merely an example, is made by the collector, the results also are likely to be systematic and comprehensive.

Much could be said on the utilitarian side of local collections. They are not made with any direct business purpose, and so far as documents, maps, and plans are concerned it obviously is the case that they have no present legal validity: otherwise they would have been retained by the solicitors and landowners directly concerned. I have seen, however, a set of maps from my own local collection produced with effect in court to prove legal obligation to maintain a thoroughfare. Although the indication on a map of a road does not verify a right of way over it, the existence of that road on a succession of maps covering a long stretch of time is a piece of evidence that a court would not neglect. That is by the way; the basic claim of the local collection is that in it is gathered and made serviceable as much of the raw materials of local history as possible.

The admission must be made that one of the difficulties in the past was that such collections were made by private individuals—and, alas, sometimes by public collectors—in a most haphazard manner. Great masses of apparently unrelated material seem to accumulate in the dwellings of some men, to the exasperation of good housewives and the faint contempt of callers who are not members of the dusty brotherhood of collectors. It was laid down years ago that the business of the collector was to get everything and to leave its appraisal to posterity[1]: which often also meant, leave its sorting and proper arrangement as well. Such altruistic, I may say egotistic, kind of collecting has its advantages if the collection passes by its maker's will to a library or other institution where it is preserved and made available, but it represents melancholy waste if, as often has happened, it is destroyed as useless junk by mourning but relieved relatives. It has no other commendation for the modern librarian. His attitude to all material is to make it live by classifying and cataloguing it to exploit it in the public interest from the first. The conclusive justification for this is that the local collection can be said to have no beginning or end; new material may arrive at any moment, and it should be assigned to its place at once.

These appear to me to be the primary and convincing reasons why in every town, village, or other group-dwelling of men, there should be some systematic effort to preserve its records. Mainly it is done by the public library which gives the name Local Collection to the gathering it makes of written, printed, graphic, and other records of the doings of its people; but it will have been assumed that several local collections

[1] *Brown's Manual of Library Economy*, p. 399, 1920.

have been enriched by the amassings of enthusiastic private collectors, who have found fascinating occupation in working upon a small definite area of the county and in endeavouring to learn everything about it from its natural conformation, soil, and climate to every form of use to which man has put it as home or working place. In doing this many objects, documents, books, prints, photographs, and so on are collected; and when these are brought into relation with other collections their interest is heightened immensely.

The assumption made here is that the collection will be in the care of a public authority, such as the urban or county library, or, in some of its material, the archives of county or town. Some definition and delimitation of the field are a necessary preliminary if success is to be attained in the most effective and economical manner. In the next chapter will be discussed the types of material to be collected. Here the question is: what areas shall be covered and who is to have custody of the collection? The hint comes from the British Records Association, which has worked on the principles that "national" material should go into a national institution, as of course the Public Record Office or the British Museum; "county" material should go into the county town, and more local material into the "town" to which it obviously belongs. It must be recognized that much local material exists in one copy only, as is obvious where deeds and other unique manuscripts are concerned;

but it is also almost as true of old books, pamphlets, maps, etc., or more modern ones that are out of print. For every library and similar institution in one county to be making a collection of the whole county must mean expensive and mutually inimical competition, from which incompleteness for all must be the result, while the cost of the items has been forced up artificially. Co-operation and division of the spoils are here as necessary as in any activity, and consultation between those concerned should achieve this. Where county collections are concerned, it may, and does, occur occasionally that the county capital is more inaccessible and much less important than some other town, and in this case the more convenient town may be preferred. What is important is that only one centre shall collect for the county generally, while every town collects specially for the material concerning itself, and perhaps its immediate suburbs.

Whether the institution which collects shall be the library, the museum, or the archive centre will usually be resolved by the simple fact that there are libraries now in all counties and in most towns, whereas museums exist only in certain towns, and archives in very few. If the three institutions exist, there should again be co-operation, in which documents having an archive character go to the archives, objects such as coins, tokens, etc., to the museum, and literary material to the library. It can be argued, of course, that for the convenience of students everything upon a subject, whatever its form, should be in one place, a perfectly logical argument in its way, but in actual practice the compromise suggested is probably the best plan. It must be assumed here, however, that the library will be the repository, and the modern reference library has been described appropriately as "the communal study, bureau of information, and muniment house." If it did not do this work of preservation, in most towns it would not be done officially at all. The official attitude in church, manor, and municipality has often been one of lamentable carelessness; often registers, minutes, and other records have disappeared from their places, and are sometimes found in the hands of private individuals. Some counties, and a few towns, to-day take systematic care of their records; most, certainly, have not done so in the past. The would-be maker of a collection has often apathy and inertia to overcome, although I think there has been more recognition of late of the value of these records. The librarian can do much to foster this if he brings his knowledge of cataloguing, classification, and filing to bear upon such documents as his own authority has accumulated and is producing.

The larger cities have developed this work greatly in the last twenty years. At Edinburgh there is an Edinburgh Room, which contains everything that can be collected upon the city, with adequate shelving, filing for pamphlets, maps, and other literary and graphic material. In the new Manchester and Sheffield

THE EDINBURGH ROOM IN THE EDINBURGH CENTRAL PUBLIC LIBRARY

[*Courtesy of the Principal Librarian*

public libraries fine apartments are devoted in the same manner. In smaller towns, Worthing is notable for its Sussex Room. These are examples amongst many. Every other library, even if it does not possess a special room, has a collection in its reference library. Some have issued catalogues of their local collections. Those from Birmingham and Gloucester are monumental, and there are many others equally worthy if not so large.

If, then, I assume that the library is the home of the local collection, it is because in general this is the case, and because this series of handbooks is for librarians. Experience tells me that this is an abiding interest of librarians; but I hope, too, that from their work others will be inspired to be interested in and to share in the perfecting of these collections.

CHAPTER II

WHAT IS COLLECTED

WE have, it is assumed, defined the area of country, the county or part of it, the town or village, about which we are to make our collection. That, it may be repeated, is the essential preliminary and a certain rigidity in keeping to that area is wisdom, not only for the reasons already suggested, but as making for completeness and clarity in our work. Thus, in my own case, Croydon collects extra-metropolitan Surrey and rigidly excludes from the collection, as such, all material dealing with that part of the county which was formerly Surrey but is now within the orbit of the London County Council. One is tempted at times to include parts of Kent, Sussex, and Hampshire, but this would, in the end, make for a certain amount of confusion and such extra-territorial collecting would be incomplete and would compete with other libraries.

This being settled, it is well to form clear views of what we intend to collect. "Everything," is the first statement of our aims, but everything is indefinable, and hardly provides a working rule. It may be better to suggest that we shall endeavour to collect every manuscript, book, pamphlet, magazine, broadside, newspaper, print, map, photograph, and other document that has been produced *about* the area, and much that has been produced *in* the area. Our aim is to include everything, except physical objects and specimens which clearly can have no place in a library, which shall illustrate the physical, natural, and civil history of the land, every change it has undergone, and every use to which its successive dwellers have put it; and this inevitably includes the history of the dwellers themselves, their development, homes, activities, crafts, amusements, products—everything from their pedigrees to their epitaphs. This material, to repeat, we get in every form.

We shall recognize, too, that our area is not static; life goes on, and to-day will be history to-morrow—a commonplace which suggests that we should collect material upon the passing hour. This raises the question: how far should the librarian *create* the material he desires to have? Should he be the copyist of records kept elsewhere, but of interest to his people, if they are not otherwise available? Should he have photographs or drawings made of current celebrations, persons, buildings which may be demolished, and other street or landscape changes? The answer is that it is probably not his business to do more than to collect, but if he can influence the production of these things, he should certainly do so. As we shall see later, librarians have energized, and indeed have often been responsible for, the forming of societies to make these records. If the librarian has time or means to do more he will undoubtedly use his own discretion as to how far he is able to go in original work. He must not do it to the detriment of his own more general work as a librarian. This obvious fact would not seem to need restatement, but there have been too many examples of librarians suddenly becoming obsessed with museum, publicity, or local collection work to the real disadvantage of the greater public they serve. Yet if the librarian does not provide the enthusiasm for the collection and make it manifest it is not likely to be supplied by others.

A general survey of the nature of the material we are to collect can be made in some such form as follows:

MATERIAL ABOUT THE AREA

1. *Manuscripts, Legal:*—These include Manorial Rolls, Deeds, Leases, Indentures, Fines, and other legal instruments which have no longer a "solicitor's value."
2. *Manuscripts, Parochial.*—Parish Registers, Vestry Minutes, Account Books, Diaries, Rate Books, etc.
3. *Manuscripts, Municipal.*—Minute Books, Agenda, Reports, Rate Books, Ledgers, Accounts, and such Deeds and other documents which do not come under 1 because they are strictly confined to agreements, etc., of the Local Authority.
4. *Manuscripts, Business.*—Minutes, Ledgers, Drafts, Plans, etc., of professional or business concerns.
5. Manuscripts of Local Authors, Letters, Autographs, etc.

WHAT IS COLLECTED

PRINTED MATERIAL

1. Histories, Topographical Accounts and Descriptions, Newspapers, Magazines, Memoirs, Biographies, Diaries.
2. Literary Records, Poems, Plays, Essays, and Novels which have a local setting or intention.
3. Church Records—Reports, Magazines, Accounts, Appeals, etc.
4. Government Records—Local Acts, Bills, Orders, Decisions, Reports of Enquiries, and every other nationally published or initiated document having a local significance.
5. Municipal (Local Government) Records—Agenda, Minutes, Reports, Calendars, Year-Books, Brochures, Guides, Notices and Incidental Papers, and other material issued by the Local Authority.

    Election Addresses, Posters, Cards, and other Canvassing material of Candidates for the Council.
6. Business Records.—Prospectuses, Sales Catalogues—especially those of auctioneers and estate agents—Advertisements, Trade Cards, Handbills, and every other form of record published by professional or business concerns in the area.
7. Music and Theatre Records—Playbills, Programmes, Souvenirs, etc.
8. Sports Records—Programmes, Records, and Accounts of Clubs and Teams.

MATERIAL PRODUCED IN THE AREA AND NOT ABOUT IT

1. Manuscript and printed works of Local Authors.
2. Speeches, Addresses, etc., delivered in the area.

3. Records and Prints, etc., of the works of Local Artists, Musicians, Scientists.
4. Records of Local Celebrities, whose fame may have been achieved elsewhere.

GRAPHIC RECORDS
1. Maps, Plans.
2. Prints.
3. Photographs.

ENGRAVED RECORDS
Some collections include Trade Tokens, Medals issued to commemorate local events, or issued locally to commemorate national ones, etc., which are perhaps "museum" objects.

Manuscripts.—Only a national library would attempt the collection of manuscripts for any wider area than a county, although possibly exceptions would be made for such libraries as the Birmingham Reference Library, which, though municipally-owned, has by its great size a more or less national character; and this may be said of the Glasgow, Liverpool, and Manchester reference libraries, and of the John Rylands Library, which competes with the older university libraries in its possession of bibliographical treasures. The ordinary local library will content itself with the documents I have indicated. Even so, they are many and will be dealt with separately and more conveniently in Chapter V.

Printed Records.—The printed records I have listed

are almost self-explanatory, and the arguments for their collection have been made sufficiently. One or two points only seem to call for comment at this stage. The net should be spread as extensively as possible, provided that system is observed from the first, and that every item as required is catalogued and classified, and, as it may need, restored, bound, and repaired. The successive editions of all publications should be sought; every librarian knows how many changes occur from edition to edition, and the latest is not always the best, or the best from the local point of view.

Local authors may need some definition. The author most obviously local, is one who is *born* in the area and pursues his work there. I think, too, that if he is merely born there and goes elsewhere, even in earliest life, he may still be recognized as local. Authors in both these classes are not always identifiable from their books. In the suburbs of London, or in near towns, this is often because the authors, from a small snobbery which every Londoner understands, prefer to date their prefaces from London rather than from, say, Croydon, Sutton, or Chingford, to which they really belong. To proceed, it is certain that the school is a most formative influence, and every writer who has attended a school in the area is usually admitted. If for no other reason, then because the school itself, a local institution, has interest in the after-life of its pupils, and both school and pupil are in my view clearly a part of local history. Other authors are not quite so easily included, but the general rule is that anyone should come in who has lived in the area long enough to be identified in some way with it; or intensely enough, which is a different matter, but quite important. Thus, we get the books of those who have held positions in municipality, church, or other public office, but who were not natives or permanently resident. The theory here is that these men have been influences upon the area, and probably have been influenced by it, and their work has been part of its life. The speeches and other writings of parliamentary candidates or representatives are worthy of consideration, and in some cases of inclusion because they have often a definitely local focus, and the parliamentary representation of a place is obviously part of its history and cannot be studied completely without such speeches. A similar argument may apply to the sermons of ministers of religion; nowadays these are often transient in their stay, but again the incumbent of a certain church is a part of its history. The methodist minister who stays only three years is perhaps different, but I would include his work actually done in the area. In none of these cases does it seem to be necessary to collect speeches or sermons made after their authors' connexion with the area has ceased; they are not in the same category as authors who are born in the area. Accounts of local trials, the speeches of counsel, and the summings-up must be kept, even if their makers have no other associations with us.

CHAPTER III

THE COST AND METHODS OF COLLECTION

COST

PROPER money provision for a local collection should be made in our estimates. The librarian would be well-advised to make this a definite item, with a sum shown which experience tells him is appropriate. This has the effect of giving continuity to the work, as a reminder to himself of the duty to see that the sum is expended wisely, and it also advises the financing authority that here is an item, inexpensive it may be, but standard and essential to the work of the library.

What the sum should be can only be settled, as suggested, by experience. All books and other forms of material which are still in print have known prices and all that is necessary is to collect them. Much local material has no standard value, and is worth exactly what the person who most wants it is prepared to pay for it. The sum, therefore, to be provided is naturally only an estimate. It will be found that as the collection grows, less will be spent on general items, and more on individual ones. This is because in the course of years we have secured all the accessible average things, and have to seek for things which grow more and more rare. We know, of course, that the first-line classics of literature in their first editions command fabulous sums. That does not make ridiculous a word about the prices of local things which, although of infinitely smaller cost, yet fetch substantially higher prices than they did originally. Examples will occur to any librarian whose collection is of some age. A pamphlet, written anonymously by John Toland, *The Description of Epsom . . . in a Letter to Eudoxia*, 1711, which bears printed on its title-page "Price 6d.", was considered cheap in 1911 at nine shillings, and is now probably worth much more. The converse is shown by books which were heavily subscribed, and therefore printed in relatively large editions. The various histories of Croydon by J. Corbet Anderson were expensive when issued, and now copies are frequent at a few shillings. Such examples are commonplace, and a study of booksellers' catalogues enables us to make some forecast of what must be paid. The matter is quite different when manuscripts are concerned. They have no price that can be fixed in any way. A selection of letters by Archbishop John Whitgift of small intrinsic value—having in them no matter of substance—because a few people probably desire to have them intensely is priced at one hundred guineas. It is this demand for the thing that creates the value, and that value is what the seller thinks the buyer can be induced to pay. In these circumstances the public librarian is at a disadvantage with the private buyer who has only himself to consider when he invests the money at his disposal. Many librarians have regretfully to pass by items which they would gladly have for this reason. It must not be supposed, however, that every rare thing must necessarily be in public care in these dangerous times. It may even be an advantage if some of them are in private hands—there may be a diffused likelihood of the escape of some in the event of air raids.

It will be concluded, from these and other considerations, that experience alone will determine what a local collection costs to gather and to maintain. It is merely desirable to have a regular estimate for it. For one county collection I know £50 is allocated to it yearly, but the sum must vary with the needs and possibilities of the place. Moreover, the collection in question has been active for nearly fifty years, and there is no leeway to make up or large gap to be filled. Even there, however, an occasional purchase has been made of a private collection, as in two instances I recall where £750 and £175 respectively were paid.

THE SEARCH FOR MATERIAL

must be continuous, and should be an organized one. Communication should be established, as already indicated, with every other library in the area, so that the field is defined, and so that each library may know what its neighbour is doing. Libraries help one another considerably now, and could do even more, if only in drawing attention to appropriate items that come to their notice in making their own searches. The most treasured item in the Croydon local collection, a *Terrier* of the thirteenth century, was noted by Mr. Ernest Axon in a catalogue which he sent to me. Transfers of items which are really in the purview of another library should be arranged wherever possible—and it generally is possible with goodwill; every librarian acting upon the assumption that the improvement of any library must benefit libraries as a whole.

In every public communication we make, our desire to obtain material should be made known. On the notepaper of several libraries appears some such legend as "The Librarian would be glad to receive gifts of written or printed books, pamphlets, documents, or prints relating to ——, or to purchase them." This has had good results. It may be made clear, too, by public notice, letters to the newspapers, and simple exhibitions that what is sought is not necessarily elaborate and expensive material as is often supposed, although this is required too, but, to speak generally, that simple letters, bills, cards, photographs, picture-postcards, broadsides, and pamphlets of all sorts are also welcomed. And, of course, the common practice of the librarian in acknowledging promptly even the smallest gift, if it needs any emphasis, needs it specially here! In all directories of booksellers, yearbooks, and so on, the collection should if possible find mention. Every bookseller should be notified that such material will be considered: this brings in many reports, some of which are necessarily productive.

The librarian must have certain discretionary powers in purchase. Where material is rare competition is keen, and not a few of us have been mortified to learn, after we have waited to consult our committee, or even chairman, that a coveted item has been "sold." Vendors are naturally not enamoured of the practice of sending things "on approval," as the delay involved may mean the loss of a sale. In some cases, however, to which again it must be said experience is the only guide, it may be possible to ask for things so to be sent; indeed, it may occasionally be necessary to adopt this course, and there must always exist the right to return things which are not what they have been represented to be. Even here some sellers preface their catalogues with words to the effect that the items are sold with all their defects and to return these may be impossible, or involve argument. To dispose of this side of the matter: the proviso is nearly always made by auctioneers in their catalogues, and this makes buying at auctions, which at the best is not a really desirable practice for a librarian, specially hazardous, unless he has examined what he wants before the sale takes place. To revert to other vendors, if we are convinced of the desirability of any item reported we should secure it by telephone or telegram, following this up, of course, with the written order which all librarians must use.

It is assumed that every catalogue that comes into a library is examined for local material. This is no mean task for some libraries, as the catalogues are many; but it is part of the sport, and definite people should be required to make the search, who appreciate all the possible headings under which what is sought may be concealed.

Relations must also be established with such authorities as are the present custodians of important records, in the hope that they will transfer them. They are often glad to be relieved of them, although this is by no means always so. The church, for example, usually preserves its parish registers with some care nowadays, even if this is not the invariable record of the past. But there are other records, such as vestry minutes, rate books, and other things which were at one time in the care of the church, and may still be housed in its muniment room, though no longer exactly in any sort of "keeping." Even here, owing to the efforts of the British Records Association, and other bodies, some care is now given in many places. Churches, it may be said in excuse, have not the money or the staffs to be record-keepers. I remember an antiquary who was allowed by his vicar to rummage in the muniment room of the church, and to "take what he wanted." Years afterwards some of the most interesting of the parish rate books of the seventeenth and eighteenth centuries were recovered one by one from private "owners"; and there are still gaps in the

COST AND METHODS OF COLLECTION 37

series. There must have been many similar examples; nor must it be assumed that every church has any living interest in these books of a form of government that has passed away. This may be the librarian's opportunity. In any case, it may be possible for the librarian to obtain copies, or at least adequate indexes, of the books retained at the church; for, ultimately, as I implied in the first sentence of this little book, the church and its records are the very foundation of local history.

The question, already mentioned, of how far the librarian should act as actual producer of the material, takes a turn here worth consideration. If the librarian cannot obtain the originals of documents, or secure copies from others, ought he to employ himself and his staff in making copies? At Walthamstow some years ago that good librarian, Mr. George E. Roebuck, copied the Parish Registers of the church there, and this gave rise to the criticism that it was scarcely the business of the librarian to engage in what must be a fairly long and not inexpensive labour when there was so much more general library work to be done. If students needed these registers, why could not they be directed to the church itself? This sort of argument would apply to many other things. It is admittedly best to collect originals if we can; but copies are certainly wanted if that cannot be done. It is assumed, of course, that such copying was part of the official employment of the librarian, because if he did it as a leisure-time work, it was the business of no one but himself. Otherwise the matter must be settled in accordance with the importance of what is copied to the collection and the staff and other means at disposal. As for the argument that the student may be sent elsewhere from the library to get what he wants, it is librarian human-nature to dislike doing this, and it is student human-nature rather to resent being sent; for clearly the convenience of both is served if the whole local material is in one place. We should make the effort to get someone else to provide the copies if we conclude that it is not our task. The various photocopying processes, the photostat for example, have made this a much more controllable matter than it was. I shall deal with that later. On the general question of copying, it is unwise to suppose there is any rule other than that of the convenience of the library service as a whole; a rule, indeed, which applies to all matters in libraries.

It is assumed that a municipal or quasi-municipal institution such as a public library receives every printed publication, map, plan, bill, and everything else put forth by the local authority. Care should be taken to see that these are complete, because it is not always the special business of "someone in the County, or City, or Town Hall" to ensure the completeness of our sets. Regular enquiry every week, or at other convenient intervals, will produce good results. It may be that the librarian can undertake the work of archivist to his authority, a post in which he is not only given custody of the records, but can be the current and official indexer of everything the authority produces, and so make himself of immense service to contemporary local administration. Here, again, not only printed matter is to be sought; many draft plans, schemes, etc., of committees never reach print, but are of great, growing interest.

The search for local deeds is a really interesting one, if it is occasionally difficult. The whereabouts of manorial and similar rolls are not always traced easily; it requires some research to discover who were the stewards, solicitors, or other guardians of these (as a rule) now invalid documents. When they are found, the characteristic caution and instinct for delay of solicitors sometimes cannot be overcome. The Master of the Rolls has been of the greatest assistance in this matter; he designates certain libraries as official repositories of manorial rolls, and such designation is a real advantage to a library. The country has now been well-surveyed from this point of view, and it is probable that in most counties the official repositories have been determined, but if our library has not been so designated an enquiry of the Master of the Rolls would be of value, since if our own manorial rolls have been allocated to some other place we should know the fact, and in that case it is possible, though by no means certain, that some adjustment might be made.

Manorial and similar feudal rolls are, however,

relatively few and rare in comparison with the innumerable legal instruments which have been drawn up for land purchase; tenancy agreements, such as leases of inns and other properties, indentures of apprenticeship, and so on. They cumber the storerooms of many solicitor firms of long standing. Thousands of them have, as already said, no validity in law to-day; are so much waste paper (or parchment), which the conservatism of the firm, or its very inertia still retains. On an occasional spring cleaning they have been sold by the sackful to gluemakers and the manufacturers of toy drums, battledores, etc., and of course at wastepaper prices. Yet in these, were they arranged with care, might be read the history of an area. Obviously, then, the librarian must make contact with all solicitors, auctioneers, estate agents, and others likely to deal in property or in legal transactions which involve the area in any way. Great tact must be exercised in doing this. The impression must be quite firmly made that the historical record and nothing else is the purpose for which these deeds are wanted. Some firms quite frankly would rather destroy deeds than have them in the custody of anyone else. Others, although they hand over documents, no longer of legal use, still make conditions as to when and to whom documents should be made available. It is usually quite possible to comply with these.

Private landowners and others in some cases prefer to retain their deeds themselves, and when the family

COST AND METHODS OF COLLECTION 41

or its head disappears these are likely to be dispersed. Here, of course, the auctioneer may be persuaded to advise the library of what is happening. In any case, whenever the sale of an old house or estate is announced we must be alert for the old deeds which may be somewhere available. This would be very specially the case where the buildings are to be demolished to make way for modern "development." Librarians of new urban and suburban areas, which to the superficial view have no history, will probably find the beginnings of their local collections in the records of some old house which has for long been the centre of the area.

It may be from such sales, or from such spring cleaning of law offices as described, but anyhow deeds do get into the hands of firms or vendors who make a business of gathering and selling them. Reports from these reach most librarians, but in any case they should be encouraged to advise upon what they find of local interest. Such agents have a keen eye for what is likely to be of value, and their prices are fixed in accordance with their view of the interest they find. It is naturally often higher than can or should be paid, and although I hold that it is not a good practice as a rule for librarians to "make offers," this is a case where a little bargaining is allowable. Something can usually be arranged. These vendors are a useful race of seekers for unconsidered trifles, and they often find what is much wanted. I recall the purchase for a few shillings from fifty miles away of a bundle of local deeds in which quite unexpectedly was found one which, in the published list of a local foundation, was recorded as having been missing for a century, and its finding completed a series. Such discoveries are the thrills of the game.

Our collection of other material begins with the local author. The life of the modern book is transient, not always unjustly, but if there is one place where it should be kept it is the library of its author's own town. Many local authors present their books, and should not be discouraged from doing so; but I am firmly of opinion that we should not solicit as gifts the work of any professional author, because we have no more right to ask without payment the work of the maker of books than we have of the maker of shelves, fuel, or soap. Local authors are often not detected as such as I showed earlier, and some are too modest to apprize us of books or other smaller works which have only a local circulation. These we want specially to collect, including, if we can get them, all works printed privately. Much can be done to encourage the feeling that the Library has an interest in cultivating and encouraging literary effort, and this will be done by reviewing such works pointedly in our bulletins, in writing notes to authors congratulating them upon the appearance of their books, in mentioning them in local lectures, and in many other ways that an ingenious librarian can devise. Indeed, if he has tact he can become in a certain way a beneficent patron of literature, or, what is much better, make the town appear to be one.

To return to the church. Every publication it puts forth of its principal activities, and its magazine, should be obtained. Here "church" covers every denomination, of course, and indeed every religious community, Christian or non-Christian, anti-Christian, or even anti-religious. Such magazines have in them much personal record, and grow in value with the years. The inset national magazine of the miscellaneous type which is often issued with such magazines need not be kept. Religious bodies are only too glad as a rule to provide the copies of their magazines, but it must be said that they are often less punctual in delivering them than is to be wished, and careful check should be kept upon them.

Men and women are more interested in themselves than in any place or thing, as is natural, and perhaps necessary. Biographies, obituary notices, and other personalia are well worth attention; the fact that any such biographies appear in print if only in the columns of local paper or church magazine makes them of importance for us. There are also diaries, notebooks, and journals which have not been published, and all kinds of other manuscript personal records, which it is sometimes possible to acquire. An effort may be made to get people to supply particulars themselves. The editor of *Who's Who*, to judge by my own case, invited the people whose notices he includes to supply him with particulars on a set form. We could adapt the idea, and when men and women come into the public eye, ask them to fill cards giving biographical particulars. These could be filed alphabetically, and in time form a local *Who's Who* of much interest. Some might refuse, but not many if the request is made tactfully. Tact would naturally suggest that those whose prominence is of the criminal kind should not be approached; their record will come to us in other ways. And, whether it is done in the way suggested or not, an index of particulars should be formed of those people who are of consequence in our area.

Many trading undertakings issue literature: catalogues, prospectuses, advertisements, and so forth. These should be obtained, and specimens of them at least should be retained. A chronological collection of such traders' advertisements is a social record of great interest. Consider this "trade card" which came into my hands in 1938: "Walter Norton Wright, Parish Clerk of Croydon, Begs to inform the Inhabitants of Croydon and its Vicinity that he procures Marriage Licences on the shortest notice." It gives a breath of the atmosphere of a world centuries away! Trade history, with the inventions which are local, may be traced in catalogues and advertisements.

Every form of activity which engages our people is our province. Bills and programmes, past and present, of theatres, concerts, dramatic, musical, literary and scientific, and other societies; the programmes of sporting organizations, team personalities and records—all these are required. An arrangement can usually be made with the managers and secretaries for a regular delivery of the items as they are published; and enquiry will often produce earlier items.

PRINTS

The collection of local prints and photographs is essential, because the picture for many purposes is better than the written word. Both subjects, however, require separate treatment. Here I may say that contact with local photographers, private as well as professional, may lead to many good additions. Another source of photographs is the Press of the area; not only should the reproductions in the newspapers be preserved, there should be an effort to persuade the editors to deposit the originals in the collection. If this fails, a selection of those of most interest can nearly always be bought. Any person who has prominence locally should be invited to have his portrait preserved. Amateur photographers should be encouraged to provide prints. The organized and most desirable source of material is a voluntary photographic society which devotes itself to making record prints and lantern slides. This and other questions will be dealt with in Chapter VII.

There does not seem to be much that we have not

touched upon, but in practice many things turn up which it is difficult to anticipate.

The essential is that we have as close contact as possible with every local society that can contribute in its own proceedings or indirectly to the record. I have found in my own case invariably that the members of such societies have valued a connexion with the libraries. It affords them advertisement, and in a certain sense, ensures—dare I say it?—some immortality for their work. The collector is indefatigable in his quest. He may have a staff, as I have, which gives lectures and addresses to societies, organizes exhibitions, and keeps a continuous outlook for local things, making continuous efforts to promote interest in the matter. Much may be done by the single collector, as I hope I have suggested. And his work has no end.

The work, it will be gathered, is not to be confined to towns of the cathedral type, or which have castles reaching back into remote antiquity. It is for every area. It is appropriate and specially necessary for quite newly-built towns. Here, while there should be the attempt, as I have already suggested, to acquire matter on the estates out of which they have developed, there should also be a scrupulous collecting of every record in every possible form of the growing of the district actually going on: records of the sales of land, its plotting out for roads and buildings, plans, accounts of the naming of the roads, the names and such facts as may be available of the inhabitants, the development of its local government and its civic, social, and religious services. It is a most interesting field to the enterprising librarian.

FILMS: SOUND RECORDS

The cinema film is likely to be one of the records of the future. The cine camera has become a popular plaything, and with it can be taken many records of our area. The fact should be made known that our collection requires these. There are also many films made for occasional purposes by the local cinemas or by firms which use these films for advertisement purposes. They are desirable from all points of view, and a persuasive policy, perhaps with a little judicious advertisement in the library in return,[1] will induce the owners of these films—many of which have from the cinema point of view only a transient purpose, but may nevertheless have enormous future interest for the student—to give them into our keeping. If sound records can be had, so much the better. Blattnerphone, gramophone, and, although much more frail, even Dictaphone records are to be welcomed. At present, however, this side of our work is not far developed.

[1] This must, of course, be appropriate advertisement, a matter on which there is at the moment no standard beyond the convenience of the public.

CHAPTER IV

ARRANGEMENT AND CATALOGUING

THE librarian is distinguished by his ability to marshal material in the most convenient manner for expeditious use. In the local collection we presume he has a pre-designed method by which every item as it is acquired falls into its appropriate place and is made serviceable at once. The old idea that things should be collected and their treatment left to some future date is, I am convinced, thoroughly bad; it discourages all connected with the work, and especially those who make gifts and who find that entries of them are not available in catalogues, and sometimes even that what they have given cannot be found. Such delay has had serious results, and there are librarians who recall the case of an important collection being lost to a library because the would-be giver was told that an earlier gift could not be found easily.

CATALOGUING AND REGISTER OF STOCK

First, then, everything that comes in should be entered in an inventory or stock register giving its description, date of acquisition, and the source from which it comes, and an indication of where it has been

ARRANGEMENT AND CATALOGUING 49

filed. With books and pamphlets this is simple, and no doubt they will be entered by the ordinary accession, book or card, methods of the library, which are described in every librarianship manual. If, however, it is desired to keep a separate local collection stock record, there is no reason why a carefully-designed card should not serve all purposes of recording and cataloguing with all the necessary cross-references. This may serve as an example for those who have not devised one of their own. The cataloguing of *deeds* as well as their classification has been the subject of study, and has been reported upon by the British Records Association (see page 69), and before the arrangement of deeds is undertaken, what has been done by that body should be considered. It appears to me to be unfortunate that the card of standard size has been superseded for the making of entries of deeds by a larger card which requires more space and larger cabinets to contain it. The card cabinet is in danger of becoming a real incubus in the modern library, which is usually too small for its ordinary work, and cannot spare space to house great card cabinets. Our card is of standard size, approximately 5 inches wide by 3 inches deep, and it is used by the unitary method which all librarians know from its use by the Library of Congress in its card system. That is to say, one card is written with all the necessary indications of author, title, class-mark, and cross-references, and this is multiplied, and the catchword or number required for each purpose is written in the top space. Here is the master card:

S70(9) PAGET, CLARENCE GEORGE.
　　　　Croydon Homes of the Past. Croydon Public Libraries. 1937.
　　　　98 pp. 15 illus. 3 plans. 8 × 5 in.

| 8 May 1938 | G. | Author | | Appeared originally as serial in The Reader's Index, v. 36–39. |

S70(728)　　/　　Croydon Homes of the Past

EXAMPLE 1

The columns on the lower half of the card are used for (1) the date the item is received; (2) G = gift, P = purchased; (3) the giver or vendor; and (4) notes of any necessary particulars.

The indications for added entries which we have mentioned are on the bottom line. The top line is left blank it will be noted. This first card will file under Paget, the author. The book will be arranged on the shelves at the class-number S70(9), as shown, with (in this case) all other books on the history of Croydon.

In modern "dictionary" cataloguing such a book would be entered under (1) its author, (2) its title, and (3) its subject or subjects in one alphabet, as are the words in a dictionary. If, then, a copy of this card is provided with the title on the top line and another with the subject, and all three cards are inserted alphabetically in a cabinet amongst other cards they form a full index to the particulars and place of the book; example 1 is the author card, and the additional cards may be shown:

Croydon homes of the past			

S70(9) PAGET, CLARENCE GEORGE
    Croydon Homes of the Past. Croydon Public Libraries. 1937.
    98 pp. 15 illus. 3 plans. 8 × 5 in.			

8 May 1938	G.	Author O	Appeared originally as serial in The Reader's Index, v. 36–39.
S70(728)	/	Croydon Homes of the Past	

EXAMPLE 2

The alternative kind of catalogue is in two parts:

(1) The author catalogue.
(2) The subject (or classified) catalogue.

52 LIBRARY LOCAL COLLECTIONS

Croydon				

S70(9) PAGET, CLARENCE GEORGE.
    Croydon Homes of the Past. Croydon Public Libraries. 1937.
    98 pp. 15 illus. 3 plans. 8 × 5 in.				

8 May 1938	G.	Author	○	Appeared originally as serial in The Reader's Index, v. 36–39.
S70(728)		/	Croydon Homes of the Past	

EXAMPLE 3

Croydon Residences.				

S70(9) PAGET, CLARENCE GEORGE.
    Croydon Homes of the Past. Croydon Public Libraries. 1937.
    98 pp. 15 illus. 3 plans. 8 × 5 in.				

8 May 1938	G.	Author	○	Appeared originally as serial in The Reader's Index, v. 36–39.
S70(728)		/	Croydon Homes of the Past	

EXAMPLE 4

ARRANGEMENT AND CATALOGUING   53

The same "unit" type of card is used. The author catalogue is merely an alphabetical arrangement of such cards as example 1 above. The subject catalogue consists of copies of the card bearing the class mark on the top line. In the Jast classification, designed for a Surrey collection, the mark for Surrey is S, for Croydon 70, and the 9 in brackets is the Dewey classification number for history (but the numbers of any other scheme would do). The mark is added on the top line, thus:

S70(9)				
S70(9) PAGET, CLARENCE GEORGE. Croydon Homes of the Past. Croydon Public Libraries. 1937. 98 pp. 15 illus. 3 plans. 8 × 5 in.				
8 May 1938	G.	Author	O	Appeared originally as serial in The Reader's Index, v. 36–39.
S70(728) / Croydon Homes of the Past				

EXAMPLE 5

The number from Dewey for Residences is 728, and this is added to S70 in order that this aspect of the book may be catalogued, thus:

54   LIBRARY LOCAL COLLECTIONS

S70(728)			

S70(9) PAGET, CLARENCE GEORGE.
  Croydon Homes of the Past. Croydon Public Libraries. 1937.
  98 pp. 15 illus. 3 plans. 8 × 5 in.			

8 May 1938	G.	Author	Appeared originally as serial in The Reader's Index, v. 36–39.
S70(728) / Croydon Homes of the Past			

EXAMPLE 6

These cards are filed under the numbers, and this has the effect of inserting them amongst other entries on Croydon history and Croydon homes. To this subject form of catalogue a subject *index* is necessary, which may be another sequence of cards, or be an alphabetical list in a book; for this book we are considering the index entries would be:

   ·Croydon, history S70(9)
   Residences, Croydon S70(728)
   Croydon, residences S70(728)

These cards are given here, as I have said, merely for those considering the subject newly. All cataloguing nowadays should follow the Anglo-American code as

ARRANGEMENT AND CATALOGUING

to form and fulness of entries. The cards could be adapted, I believe, to almost any form of material. Two examples, one of a deed, the other of a lantern slide, will suffice to prove this.

dS86	Riddenhurst, Manor of.			
(333)	Sale of Manor of Riddenhurst, etc. From Mercer of Cranley to Butt of Same. 28 Jan. 1672.			
Oct. 1917	P.	Baldwin	5s.	The manor of Riddenhurst, 300 acres in Cranley, Hascombe and Shalford and other lands in Hascombe and Cranley.
Cranley / Hascombe / Mercer / Butt				

EXAMPLE 7.—Master Card for a Deed

For *full* indexing, it will be seen that six copies of this card are required under Riddenhurst, Cranley, Hascombe Mercer, Butt, and (if the subject catalogue is used) under S86(333) (the lower case "d" means "deed," of course). Few libraries, however, would, or could, afford so many, and local knowledge would decide what were the essential entries. It may be preferred to deal with deeds in the manner recommended by the British Records Association, to which I have already referred, in Chapter V.

The cataloguing of a negative, or any kind of print, much resembles this; and maps, entered under the cartographer, by the standard rule, may also go on such cards; in each case, of course, with appropriate cross-references. If when we have "carded" all material

---

1S YOUNG, W. P.				
House with dated sundial, The Plain, Wandsworth. Lantern slide from W.P.Y.'s negative. 4 July, 1904.				
8 Jan. 1905	G.	Photographer		
Wandsworth / Plain, The / Sundials / Surrey				

EXAMPLE 8.—Master Card for a Lantern Slide

thus, we arrange them by their headings in one alphabetical sequence, we shall have a sound, simple index to our collection.

Although selective or abbreviated cataloguing may be advisable in some places and for many classes of book in an organization like the public library where much of the stock is transient, for the local collection, whatever form of catalogue is adopted, full bibliographical cataloguing is the best, if, as is presumed, the collection is in the hands of librarians who have the requisite cataloguing knowledge. The entry should show, then, the name of the person or persons, or body of persons (or organization, which is much the same thing), responsible for the existence of the work; its date; place of origin and publisher; the number of pages; its size in inches (or centimetres, if that method is preferred); the number of illustrations coloured and uncoloured; and of maps, plans, tables; the presence of bibliographies, how long they are, and of what kind (classified, annotated, or otherwise); the binding, and whether it is original; the first price if known; the defects if any of the copy, and whether they always existed or appear to be the result of loss or accident. It is always to be assumed that such catalogues are complete inventories of local material.

CLASSIFICATION

The arrangement of the collection should be a simple matter to the librarian when once he has determined his guiding principle. That will depend upon his choice between place and subject as the basis of his classification. It may be put as a question: does the enquirer want all the material about a given place, or does he want all the material about a subject in the given place? Or, it may be put this way: does he want an account of a ward in a town involving every object and circumstance in it, or does he want (say) an account of architecture of the town? In a county collection, does he want all the material relating to Richmond in Surrey, or that relating to the churches of Surrey? On this will be determined whether the collection is arranged in this order:

>Surrey
>>Abinger
>>>General
>>>Philosophy
>>>Religion
>>>Sociology, etc.
>>
>>Ashstead
>>>divided, as before
>>
>>Bookham
>>>divided, as before
>>
>>etc.

or in this:

>General Works—Surrey.
>Philosophy—divided by the places in the county alphabetically or in some other way.
>Religion—divided as Philosophy.

Both methods have their advocates, but it may be urged that the very idea of the local collection is locality, or topography, and, on this argument, place and not subject must prevail in the basic order. On the other hand, the arrangement advocated by L. Stanley Jast, and used by him to arrange the prints of

ARRANGEMENT AND CATALOGUING 59

the Photographic Survey and Record of Surrey uses the subject method with place sub-divisions.

If a standard classification is used, the notation *can* be adjusted to mark the local collection, but it must necessarily be lengthy. In the Dewey Decimal Classification, for example, London is 914.21, and if we were to "divide by the classification" we should get such numbers as

914.21(726) London churches

and this symbol has taken us only to London as a whole, with its churches as a whole. It is usually found economical to use an arbitrary symbol for the area, i.e. L = London, and then L726 is the much shorter number that will indicate London churches if we use Dewey sub-division of our subjects. It is usual for librarians to use the initial letter of the county or town name to mark their collection as a whole, and then to sub-divide topographically first, in a town by the wards or parishes, and then to re-divide by the subject numbers from the Dewey or other classification in use. This gives simple but quite effective service; thus, if again I make use of the county best known to me:

S Surrey, General.
   Hills, Streams, Roads, and other features which cross or affect the county as a whole or in several parts go here as well as material on the county as a whole.

60 LIBRARY LOCAL COLLECTIONS

The first divisions, the great parts of the county may be indicated thus:

S01   North
S011 North East
S012 North West

S02   South
S021 South East
S022 South West

S03   East

S04   West

which take material covering or concerned with these areas as a whole.

Individual towns and villages may be arranged either in hundreds, which is a good logical order; thus:

S   Surrey
S25   Wallington Hundred
S251   Banstead
S252   Beddington
S253   Carshalton
S254   Croydon
S255   Purley
S256   Waddon
         etc.

or, as is found more simple and almost as effective, in one straight alphabetical order of all places. The sample that follows shows three modes of notation; i.e. a simple alphabetical letter symbol; a straight continuous number; and a decimal number which marks and divides the initial letters of the place names alphabetically.

S				Surrey
	SA	S1	S1	Abinger
	SAD	S2	S11	Addington
	SADD	S3	S12	Addlestone
	SAL	S4	S13	Albury
	SALF	S5	S14	Alford
	SAS	S6	S15	Ash
	SASH	S7	S16	Ashstead
	SB	S8	S2	Bagshot
	SBA	S9	S21	Balham
	SBAN	S10	S22	Banstead
	SBAR	S11	S23	Barnes

and so on.

These numbers are divided by the Dewey Decimal classification in the following examples:

S	Surrey—topography generally
S(016)	Bibliography
S(2)	Religion
S(352)	Local government
S(37)	Education—schools
S(427)	Dialect
etc.	
SAD	Addington
SAD(352)	Local Government
SAD(726)	Church
SAD(728)	Palace
SAD(79)	Sports
SAD(9)	History
SAD(92)	Biography

and so on, as the material requires.

When the collection is limited to a town the notation problem is even more simple. Here we can have:

B	Bylston	
B1	North	
B11		Alden Ward
B12		Borden Ward
B13		Calthrop Ward
B14		Wilford Ward
B2	South	
B21		Alexander Ward
B22		Bensham Ward
B23		Whitehorse Manor Ward
B3	East	
B4	West	

Sub-divided in the same manner as the North and South Wards, and redivided by Dewey subject numbers as shown for the county numbers.

This method will be found to work, and for all material. It is desirable, however, to separate the various *forms* of it, and a lower case letter (arbitrarily chosen perhaps) may precede the class mark to individualize the various collections:

bS252 a broadside;
dS252 a deed;
eS252 an engraving or other print;
fS252 a folio book;
lS252 a lantern slide;
mS252 an original MS., not a deed;
nS252 a negative;
pS252 a pamphlet;
qS252 a quarto book;
sS252 a survey photographic print;
tS252 a token.

f, q, and p are, of course, the common cataloguing signs for folio, quarto, and pamphlet, and as these are all shelved separately as a rule, their use is obvious. The use of the other signs becomes clear when we consider methods of filing our collection.

This chapter consists only of elementary suggestions which can be followed in treatises on classification. It will be found on examination that the subject has interested many librarians who have made their suggestions in the various library journals. A book worth the attention of students is *The Camera as a Historian*, 1916,[1] under which title H. D. Gower, L. Stanley Jast, and W. W. Topley made a detailed study of photographic surveys and how to classify, catalogue, and file the prints, amongst other matters. The classification there proposed is a subject one, used on the ground that the subjects of photographs are often of small details, as stiles, gates, architectural details, windows, inn-signs, etc., and that the topographical interest is secondary to the subject one. This the reader may like to pursue for himself in the book cited.

[1] Sampson Low.

CHAPTER V

DEEDS AND MANUSCRIPTS

In a broad, general sense this book is concerned throughout with what may be called local archives, and the foundation of all archive collections are the written documents which are comprehended under the portmanteau word, deeds. It is, however, only in a cursory, indicative manner that we can deal with these, because their full treatment involves a special technical equipment, in which in varying degrees are employed the studies of palaeography and diplomatic, ancient land tenures, manorial and feudal courts and customs, classical and medieval languages, dialects and contractions, as well as other most fascinating matters which are beyond our scope here. Fortunately in modern times a number of devoted workers have given much study to the subject, and have been active in arousing practical public interest in it. They are embodied in the British Records Association, which encourages the study from all standpoints, and through its Records Preservation Section has issued a series of tentative but most suggestive reports on the methods of handling and exploiting documents; and these are useful not only to the expert, they are invaluable to the beginner and the amateur.

The librarian is concerned to collect deeds, and we

have already shown in Chapter III in what manner he may proceed, but he should also get his authority to join the British Records Association, because through it by exchanges and transfers many deeds have been placed in libraries or repositories in their right localities. It is also a source of expert information on all matters relative to them.

Under the Law of Property Act, 1922, as amended by the Act of 1924,[1] there is special provision for the care of manorial documents. These are defined as "court rolls, surveys, maps, terriers, documents, and books of every description relating to the boundaries, franchises, wastes, customs or courts of a manor, but do not include the deeds or other instruments provided for evidencing the title to a manor; 'manor' includes a lordship or reputed lordship; and 'lord of the manor' includes a person entitled to manorial documents." There it is directed that these shall remain in the care of the lord of the manor for the time being, and that he must not damage or destroy them. The Master of the Rolls may demand to know if such documents are in proper custody, and are being properly preserved. Clause (4) provides—

That the Master of the Rolls may direct that any manorial documents which, in his opinion, are not being properly preserved, or which he is directed by a lord of the manor to deal with under this sub-section, shall be transferred to the Public Record Office, or to any public library, or

[1] 15 Geo. V, ch. 5, Sched. Z, Sect. 2.

museum, or historical or antiquarian society, which may be willing to receive the same, and if the same shall be transferred to any public library or museum or historical or antiquarian society, the governing body thereof shall thereafter have the custody thereof and shall be responsible for the proper preservation and custody thereof.

It is also provided in the Act that any person may have right of access free of charge to the documents, and "to have the same kept in a proper state of preservation; in particular the lord of the manor shall remain entitled to require the same to be produced to him, or in accordance with his directions, free of cost."

The Master of the Rolls may make rules to give effect to the Act, and may vary or revoke them as he finds necessary. Accordingly such rules were made in 1925.[1] These direct that the lord of the manor shall keep his documents, when not in use, safely in receptacles approved by the Master of the Rolls, directs the lord of the manor to report on their condition to the Deputy Keeper of the Public Records, who may require him to repair them "so far as he is able," and also directs the "lord" to keep the Deputy Keeper informed of any change in the ownership of the deeds. When the documents are transferred to a library or similar authority, that authority must send a list of them to the Deputy Keeper, on a form to be obtained

[1] Statutory Rules and Orders, 1925, No. $\frac{1310}{L.49}$, Law of Property, H.M. Stationery Office, 1926, Price 1d.

from him. The authority must see that they are kept in suitable receptacles; that is to say, a fireproof strong-room is required as a condition of recognizing a library as a depository for documents. The authority must not transfer the documents, except by the consent of the Master of the Rolls. During reasonable hours they must be available not only to the lord of the manor, but also to any person interested in land enfranchised by the Law of Property Act, 1922, or under the Copyhold Acts of 1841 and 1894, "on payment of the fees authorized by those Acts." (On this it may be remarked that *public* libraries do not charge fees.) Other persons who desire to inspect them must have the consent of the lord of the manor or the Master of the Rolls; nor must documents be copied except under the supervision of some responsible person.

Our first business, then, if we are newly contemplating the collecting of such documents, is to communicate with the Master of the Rolls at the Public Record Office, Chancery Lane, W.C.2, so that we may learn if some other library or institution has been designated to receive the documents of our area, and if not, if ours may be considered. If some other place has been favoured, relations with it for mutual assistance should be established if possible.

The main problems are the physical condition of a document and, where needed, its repair; its classification and cataloguing; its storage; its use either directly or by means of the copies which should always be made of unusually important deeds; and the provision of transcriptions or translations.

When a deed is received it will as a matter of routine be examined as to its condition, completeness, the presence of seals, etc. Seals are often of considerable importance, and must be handled with great care as they are vulnerable. Deeds which are dirty should be dusted and brushed. If strong enough, they can be damped and placed in a light press to flatten them. If they have faded, they can be submitted to a restoring process by the use of gallic acid in the proportion of one part acid to one hundred parts water, but great care should be exercised in the process. Repairs may be done to minor documents by backing them, if the text is on one side, with silk or linen. When the deed is of much value it is well to get it repaired by the Public Record Office, or some other expert authority.

Large deeds could be filed flat in the manner in which plans or similar documents are preserved, but these often occur in groups, and are required in that order. This has led to the practice of using tape to tie those which have a common interest into bundles, and these bundles are filed in boxes.

In my own practice all deeds are placed in folders after any treatment to strengthen or preserve them, and go into the vertical file, but are first placed in envelopes of strong manilla paper instead of folders. The deeds are usually folded when received, and suffer

DEEDS AND MANUSCRIPTS

no apparent harm from remaining folded. On the envelope can be written the call-marks or other indications, and it is usual to paste a copy of the catalogue entry of the deed upon it; this gives a precise account of the contents, and often prevents unnecessary handling of the deed itself.

It is advisable to have the most important deeds copied, so that true copies are available for ordinary use, and will exist if calamity overtakes the original. The photostat, micro-film, and other methods exist for this purpose, and copying is relatively inexpensive. Some libraries maintain a photostat or other equipment, and these will copy for other libraries, as Birmingham Reference Library most characteristically and excellently does.

Transcriptions are of the utmost value in the local collection. Even if it can be affirmed that the real student of historical matter must be able to decipher the original, in fact many cannot, and in any case his work is greatly facilitated by accurate translations, and through them the ordinary man finds an interest otherwise denied him. It is therefore advisable that full copies in modern English be made of all deeds which are not in that language.

The classification and cataloguing of deeds may now be undertaken, as far as possible, on the lines laid down tentatively by the British Records Association; although, as I have already complained, I think a mistake was made in using a card 6 ×

4 inches in dimensions instead of the standard 5 × 3 inches for the inventory. In cataloguing, the information required concerns: the date of the deed; the nature of the transaction; names of parties; consideration; subject, including place names; tenure; witnesses; seals; marginal notes and endorsements. The main entry is made under the place name, and other information, which is shown on the unit card is made by cross-references. The British Records Association's model is shown on page 71. Both the back and front of the card are used. Cross references, called in the code in question "continuation cards," are made for: (1) *personal names* under the heading of *parties and witnesses*; (2) places where place names other than that in the heading occur; (3) seals. A card of different colour is suggested for each type of cross-reference. Seals can be catalogued from the points of view of date, place, and reference to the document to which it belongs, as well as owner, form, shape, size, colour, material, method of attachment, design, legend, and condition. Each of these conveys an acceptable piece of information, but the process of making fourteen entries for a possible seal does not seem to be a likely one. The ordinary cataloguer would enter them under owner, and under the document to which they belong.

I have already shown in Chapter IV that deeds can be catalogued simply, but quite practically, on the unit principle.

Front

Place or Places	
Date	Ref.
Parties	Description of Instrument *See Continuation Card* Subject of Transaction
Witnesses	Field Names, etc.
Seals	Consideration
Language, Material, and Size	

Back

Signatures	Endorsements:
	(a) Witnesses to Sealing
Remarks	(b) Witnesses to Livery of Seisin
	(c) Other Endorsements

Literary manuscripts, which are not in roll or folded form, such as the manuscripts of the works of local authors, should be bound strongly and appropriately as books. For this I would prefer a strong cloth or buckram to leather, as being more durable for works that are not likely to be much handled. Each volume could be provided with a linen-covered cardboard slip-in case. Cataloguing of such MSS. is as for books.

The filing of autograph letters may be done by dropping them loosely into classified folders in the vertical file. Although some authorities condemn it, I would attach them by a "bank-paper" hinge to a stout paper mount of quarto size before placing them in folders. They are thus kept rigid and free from the dangers of crumpling, and can be turned on the hinge so that both sides of the sheet can be read.

I am only too conscious that this is a most cursory treatment of a subject which in the works of Hubert Hall, Hilary Jenkinson, Charles Johnson, V. H. Galbraith, and others, has received full and scholarly treatment. The beginner would be well advised to read the little booklet on *The Care of Documents*, by Charles Johnson, and *Archive Administration*, by Hilary Jenkinson.

CHAPTER VI

GRAPHIC RECORDS

IN the local collection the work of the painter and engraver is included only from the record point of view. It is true that the library should be made as attractive as possible, and that good pictures on our walls conduce to that end. If these pictures are of local subjects, or are by local artists, or are both, so much the better, with a warning against keeping any picture too long in one place. There is not much wall-space in the average library, and what there is is not always good for the display of pictures, because the lighting has been devised for other purposes. There is also the aesthetic truth that for their adequate display pictures should have sufficient space and be right in relation to the walls on which they rest. A crowd of local pictures, placed together from a subject point of view, may have great interest, but as a beautifier of the room in which it is placed will not be successful. If an exhibition room is to be had, this will not matter, but, as a librarian, I deprecate the loading of walls with pictures, which as pictures will rarely be of first quality, in a building which is intended to exploit books. It is only when there is no art gallery in which the work of the local artist or pictures of the locality can be preserved that the librarian is justified in entering this field. Out of the disadvantage of "no museum and no art gallery," does arise the advantage that such material, graphic and literary, as exists is to be found in one place.

From these considerations it will be assumed that what we collect are pictures in any grade of artistic merit, or in any process, which depict our area. Many of them will be by amateurs, and be what Mr. Jast has called, by an expressive terminological-contradiction, "artistic atrocities," but here as everywhere in this work it is by the setting of them side by side with other works that facts are learned which may be otherwise unobtainable. It is preferable that pictures be unframed for this collection, but framed ones are often received. These can be stored in racks in which they stand upon their edges. The corners of the frames should be protected with triangular covers made of paper folded thickly, much in the manner in which corners of books are sometimes protected. This is necessary, as nothing is more unsightly than frames chipped and ragged. To the ends of the pictures a label bearing the number and location of the picture should be affixed. Another method is that of vertical baize-covered screens, on both sides of which the pictures are hung close together. Such screens can be on castors running in grooves on the floor, and pack side by side like the cases in a rolling bookstack. The screens are numbered and the index of pictures refers to this number. Few libraries, however, can afford these. Unframed pictures, in oils, should be placed in folders and filed in flat boxes or drawers similar to those suggested for maps or plans. This procedure may be followed for large water-colours, but it is best to protect the painted surface with a sheet of paper which may be attached to the back and folded over the painted surface, and of course be large enough to cover it completely.

Smaller water-colours should all be placed in cut-out mounts with a paper cover as for larger ones. They can be set into vertical files, but should be placed first in envelopes or folders, and the remarks about dividers apply specially here. Because of their greater liability to damage than other pictures, they are often filed in boxes which lie flat on shelves. Most of these remarks apply to original pencil or pen drawings.

The local *print* forms a most engaging subject for the collector. As a librarian, I often think too engaging, as many a desirable book has been mutilated by the rapacity of collectors. This suggests what is a fact, that a large number of topographical prints have been extracted from books. We ourselves would extract them from volumes which are defective, worn-out, or otherwise no longer useful as books; but there is quite a traffic in prints from live books. To digress for a moment: we have to supervise with special care our illustrated books, because the tactics are skilful of the print-thief; he can sit at a reading table, remove a plate, and work it under his waistcoat under the very eyes of a not particularly observant staff. Nor is he deterred by our identification stamps, even if they perforate or emboss; faking is well understood by these gentry.

That is by the way. It will be helpful if we familiarize ourselves with the various processes of the print engraver: the wood engraving, Baxtertype, etching, dry point and soft-grained, line-engraving, mezzotint, herkotype, aquatint, lithography, and so down to modern process block printing of illustrations. It is beyond our plan here to attempt this, because there are excellent books to which every librarian has access on all of them, and some knowledge of this sort is part of his ordinary equipment.

When prints are received they should be cleaned, restored if necessary, and, usually I think, mounted. Much care must be exercised, as print-surfaces are often quite fragile, and no collector of, say, wood-engravings would allow anyone to finger the surface of his prints. C. W. F. Goss, in an excellent study written some years ago,[1] advises that prints which have foxed through damp should be treated at once, by soaking them, if their texture will bear it, in a bath of weak sodium hypochlorite. Ink stains he would remove with a one-to-six solution of salts of lemon with water, and when the patch is dry would tone it up with a little weak tea; mildew is disposed of by warming the print slowly, and then brushing the spots with a sable hair

[1] "Methods of Producing and Preserving Prints, *Library Association Record*, vol. 17, pp. 265-94, 332-62.

brush; grease and candle spots by placing the print downward on glass and dabbing the spots with cotton wool soaked in benzine, sulphuric ether, or naphtha, and the grease will evaporate with the spirit; petrol of high grade can be used for very bad prints, but care must be taken to do it in the open air, well away from any fire; and sometimes grease spots can be removed by placing a print between blotting paper and pressing it gently but continuously with a hot iron, renewing the blotting paper at intervals; bloodstains are removed by a bath of sodium chlorinate; brown fox marks will usually disappear if spirits of wine or ammonia are dabbed over them; and fly marks can be touched off with a solution of peroxide of hydrogen. These are the most common defects of prints. Such treatment as is indicated here is not to be undertaken without considerable preliminary practice, which, as Mr. Goss advises, should be carried out on prints of no value before the prints of the collection itself are attempted. I am inclined to suggest, when it can be afforded, that the work should be confided to a professional restorer.

The mounting of prints of any value should be by the method suggested for water-colours, and their filing may be much the same. Ordinary photo-process prints which are on art paper do not need elaborate mounts, but these should be of uniform size. This insistence upon uniformity is to make prints fit conveniently into the filing system, but the second use of it may be even more important. It facilitates their display; because a series of frames can be made with moveable backs which can be used to exhibit a frequently-changed series of drawings or prints. Such exhibitions are not only of public interest; they invite gifts. Here, indeed, is one of the difficulties of the librarian; he has little space for showing his treasures, yet he knows that those who give prints or other items are disappointed if they cannot be shown publicly. If we can provide in our vestibules show-cases on which some exhibition can be made, it will be an advantage. The contents of these should be constantly changed.

CHAPTER VII

PHOTOGRAPHIC AND REGIONAL SURVEY RECORDS

THE camera has reinforced all forms of record work immeasurably. The value of the photographic print lies in its general fidelity, although camera-untruth is quite common, the ease with which it is made, the popularity of the work, and the possibility, if negatives are collected too, of multiplying copies to any extent. To-day there are cameras in almost every home, some of considerable quality, and amongst them are cine-cameras. They are often used merely for personal records, and often without purpose. The advent of the miniature camera, however, has given a fillip to good work. If these cameras could be organized and their use directed to the making of systematic surveys of our areas many advantages would follow. That it should be done is more necessary now than at any previous time because change is so rapid that the countenance of a town is often completely changed in a year or two, and modern transport has affected life so that much of the countryside of the old England men of fifty knew will be something of which their grandsons will be unable to form even a vague notion.

It was Sir Benjamin Stone, whose photographic

collection is in Birmingham Public Libraries, who advocated the use of the camera in this way fifty years ago, and a series of his record photographs was published as a demonstration. Certain local societies took the hint, and the public library came into the field. The first librarian to realize it on a scale commensurate with its importance was Louis Stanley Jast, who, with the aid of some enthusiastic members of his Libraries Committee, formed in 1902 what was called the Photographic Survey and Record of Surrey. It consisted of all the professional, and still more, in the nature of things, the amateur, photographers who could be roped in; and at that time photographic materials were relatively cheap, and amateur-photography was a quite popular pastime. The society was organized on county lines, with well-considered rules and a nominal subscription; and it began with great enthusiasm. The county was divided into areas, and representatives were appointed who themselves would photograph and encourage others to do so in the respective areas. A central council, popularly elected, produced cards of membership which were the authorization that could be presented to property-owners, vicars, and others whose buildings or other things it was desired to record. It also arranged—this being primarily the work of Mr. Jast—a classification of the subjects wanted, such as antiquities, architecture, geological sections and formations, characteristic landscapes, natural history subjects, passing events, celebrations, games,

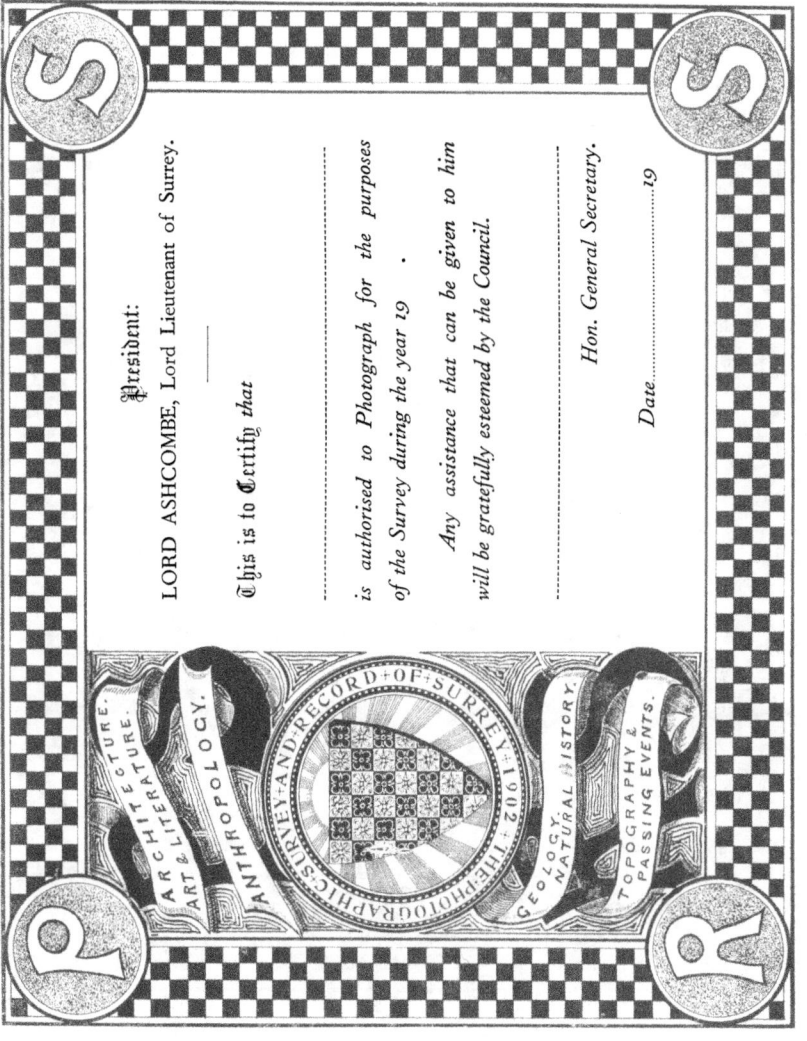

MEMBER'S CARD, THE PHOTOGRAPHIC SURVEY AND RECORD OF SURREY

pastimes, and persons. Reproductions of unique works of art, or works of art about Surrey or by Surrey artists, were also wanted. Indeed, the scheme envisaged the photographing of everything that would create, as it were, a complete visual encyclopaedia of the past and present of the county.

Some simple principles emerged. It was desired that prints should be in a permanent process, at that time the platinotype was preferred to the silver-print, and although the processes have changed with time the principle of permanence prevails still; but, it was the rule to accept a poor and impermanent print if no other was available, for it could sometimes be copied, and an imperfect record, if accurate, was of course better than none. Again, the prints were to be fully "documented"; each photographer was asked to supply precise information as to the whereabouts of the subject photographed, the date, the compass point from which it was taken, the name and address of the photographer and the society, if any, of which he was a member. It was recognized that much of the value of the print depended upon the accuracy of these particulars. In order that they might be uniformly dealt with, each member of the Survey was provided with a number of labels, as shown on p. 82, which may be familiar to the reader from its appearance in other books. One is attached to every print, and this enables the Survey Secretary (who is a member of the Libraries staff, acting here in an unpaid capacity) to record in

LIBRARY LOCAL COLLECTIONS

THE PHOTOGRAPHIC SURVEY AND RECORD OF SURREY

Slip to accompany Prints and Lantern Slides

It is requested that you will fill in the required particulars on this slip and forward it and your print or lantern slide to the Hon. Survey Sec., Public Library, Town Hall.

ACCESS TO COLLECTION.
The Collection is permanently housed at the Public Library, Town Hall, Croydon, under regulations making it accessible to the public.

COPYRIGHT.
The Copyright of a photograph remains the property of the contributor, unless specially ceded to the Association.

Class No.*	Locality	No. of 6-in. Ord. mp. ‡ sheet	Subject		Survey No.*
Size ___ plate	Process	Date Photographed	Time ___ a.m. p.m.	¶Compass Point	Date Received*
Description					
Name and Address of Contributor			Member of the following Society (if any)—		

Use one form for each print. Write clearly. * Leave blank
Photographic Survey and Record of Surrey. ¶ The compass point towards which camera is pointing.
Make description brief.

a ledger the receipt of the print. The part within the black line is cut off and pasted upon the card upon which the print is mounted. It will be noted, as one other principle, that the copyright of any print is the property of the member, and that only by his permission may it be reproduced. Usually, however, this is not pressed, but it protects the professional photographer, who contributes, from exploitation. All prints should be mounted, and it is important that mounts should be of uniform size, or of not more than two sizes, in order that they may fit conveniently into uniform volumes, cabinets, or boxes. The sizes which experience has proved to be convenient are, for all ordinary prints $10\frac{1}{4} \times 12\frac{7}{8}$ inches, and for the smaller number of very large ones 17×14 inches. The sizes in question are those into which the much larger manufacturers' sizes can be cut with the least waste. If prints are centred, approximately, on these mounts, and the label is placed in the left top corner, the record is complete and ready for use. Considerable thought had to be given to the material of the mount, as it must be free from anything in its composition which may set up chemical action in the print, and for the same reason the adhesive used was studied. Our experience proves that Cosmos board, storm grey in tint, and of plain finish, which cuts conveniently to the sizes laid down, has stood the test of many years.[1]

[1] Messrs. Spalding and Hodge, Ltd., Drury House, Russell Street, W.C.2.

The mounting process of the Adhesive Dry Mounting Company[1] is probably better than any other, and is certainly to be preferred to any paste or gum.

The arrangement of the mounted photograph will of course be by the classification applied to the local collection generally. Enough has been said perhaps about arrangement by *place*, but a careful study may be made of Mr. Jasts's classification by *subject*, which is given in *The Camera as Historian*. A brief outline may be interesting:

01–47 Topography. [These numbers are taken from the 6-inch sheets of the Ordnance Survey of Surrey, but larger counties have more than 47 sheets, and for such counties the numbers can be divided decimally.]
48 Art.
49 Literature.
50 Geology.
51 Palaeontology.
52 Zoology.
53 Botany.
53.7 Horticulture and Agriculture.
54 Architecture
55 Antiquities.
56 Meteorology.
57 Passing Events.
58
59

[1] 27 Fetter Lane, London, E.C.4.

PHOTOGRAPHIC RECORDS

(60) to (99). The county divided by towns and districts. This is for the arrangement of material which does not fit conveniently into 01–47. For example, it may be used to sub-divide 498 maps and plans. The bracket is used to indicate that the numbers are sub-divisions of subject numbers. When collections of *books* are being arranged the numbers (60) to (90), but without the brackets, may be the arrangement of them; thus:

> S60 Surrey. General.
> S61 North.
> S62 South.
> S63 East.
> S64 West.
> S65 Barnes.
> S66 Carshalton.
> S70 Croydon.
> etc.

The practice Mr. Jast followed was to sub-divide these numbers by a Dewey number enclosed in brackets in the manner described on page 61.

Each of the main headings is sub-divided, thus:

> 48 Art.
> 481 Paintings of the county.
> 481.5 Paintings not representing the county, but by county artists.
> 481.9 Other paintings.
> 482 Sculpture.
> 489 Portraits.

There are occasional special tables for the further sub-division of special classes of matter, such as under 01–47 Topography, special features; thus:

  264   South-East Surrey.
  264(1) Water views, rivers, etc.
  264(2) Woods, parks, etc.
  264(3) Hills and valleys,
  and so on;

and thus of 489, Portraits:

  489A of the subject.
      B of his parents.
          B2 father; B3 mother, etc.
      C other members of his family.
          C2 brothers; C3 sisters, etc.
      D wife.

Such an arrangement needs both an index of subjects and of places, which may be kept most conveniently on cards. If a *place* arrangement of prints is used, it is self-indexing so far as place is concerned, but an index to the subject numbers is required. This, if the Dewey classification furnishes the sub-divisions under place, is merely the printed index of that scheme itself, although in some libraries a more selective index is made specially.

The filing of the mounted prints is done in various ways. There are:

(1) *The loose-leaf ledger method.*—Here the mounts are perforated as are the sheets in a sheaf catalogue or

in a loose-leaf ledger, and they are secured by a thong or other means, well known in that method, into covers, thus making volumes into which additions may be inserted.

(2) *Box filing.*—The use of boxes which can be made to lie flat on shelves and have a hinged lid, and a front that falls outward to enable the mounts to slide in and out, is an inexpensive and popular method, especially for small collections. The size of the box is that of the mount, allowing at least a quarter of an inch "play" around it to prevent damage of the most vulnerable part of the mount, the edges. The box should bear a xylonite label holder on the side facing outwards when it rests on the shelf, and on the label it holds will of course be written the inclusive class-numbers of the prints in it.

(3) *The vertical file*, in my view, surpasses every other method for the housing of mounted prints, especially for the smaller of the two sizes of mount recommended, which fits comfortably into the standard foolscap vertical file. Steel cabinets run more easily, and are more fire-resistant than wooden ones. In the file the mounts stand on edge, the label upwards of course, and facing the user. This method is much more convenient and rapid in use than the others, and when it is used properly insertions and withdrawals are made with the utmost ease. The drawbacks are

that drawers of mounted photographs are heavy, and the mounts tend to become a solid block which must be separated with care when consultation takes place; otherwise the edges become frayed after a time. To prevent this, wood or millboard dividers, as wide as the mounts, but projecting a half-inch above them, should be inserted at six-inch intervals in the drawers. The projections can serve as guides, and the divider prevents the sagging together of the mounts. Another danger is friction of the print surfaces, and this is a real one. For unique or valuable prints a folder or envelope should be provided which will afford the necessary protection.

The work of the photographic survey is aided by definite programmes of work for its members. For example, whenever a new by-pass or other road is contemplated, as is often the case nowadays, the whole of the properties it is to traverse and the adjacent ones are affected. The organization can arrange for a systematic photographing of the whole of these; and to do this and similar jobs, excursions can be arranged. Most useful and agreeable excursions are arranged by some societies during week-ends or half-days, with much benefit to the collection. Regular meetings, at not oppressively frequent intervals, occasional lectures, an annual exhibition of results, and an annual report of course, are all aids to a lively form of record service.

REGIONAL SURVEYS

Somewhat akin to the Photographic Survey, but different in form, and more inclusive, is what is known as the Regional Survey. The late Professor Patrick Geddes, at The Outlook Tower, Edinburgh, was and C. C. Fagg, of Croydon, is amongst its pioneers. It may be described as an attempt to collect data, in its most scientifically accurate form, about a given area, and to record it by graphs, diagrams, plans, and, more definitely, maps. The work is undertaken by a society formed for the purpose, in some cases, and in others is a part of the local scientific or similar society. The area is chosen, and a series of outline maps of it are obtained through the Ordnance Survey. Then each regional surveyor plots on a map a definite type of information, hatching and colouring it to record his facts. Thus, the geology of the region is an obvious one; another the open spaces in public ownership; another the transport of the past, roads from the primitive trackway to the modern highway; another of railways and other lines of communication; another of the residential estates, castles, mansions; another of agriculture; another of manufactures; another of population. Some maps have historical matter only, some deal with passing things, and all are subject to constant revision, even to substitution. The maps, put together, form the most elaborate, detailed, and accurate examination of a district that it is possible to make.

90 LIBRARY LOCAL COLLECTIONS

In the case of the Croydon Regional Survey, the area is that lying within a circle having a fifteen-mile radius from the Croydon Town Hall. The work is carried out by the Regional Survey section of the Croydon Natural History and Scientific Society. An atlas of maps, kept in a binder on the loose-leaf principle, is maintained by the section in the reference library. The most complete of these maps are being published serially to subscribers, each of whom is furnished with a lettered binder into which the maps are inserted. Such a work is naturally slow in process and can never be completed, as no area can ever remain static; but that simple truth applies to most of the subjects in our local collection. To those who would follow this interesting development further we may commend a study of the actual published serial, *Regional Survey Atlas of Croydon and District*,[1] 1936 to date, and a most readable book, *An Introduction to Regional Surveying*,[2] 1900, by C. C. Fagg and G. E. Hutchings.

MISCELLANEOUS PHOTOGRAPHS

All the photographs that come into the possession of the library are not contributed by survey societies. Their treatment is, however, according to the same plan, but in all records some distinguishing symbol can

[1] Croydon Natural History and Scientific Society.
[2] Cambridge University Press.

be used to identify them. It would be best, I think, to make them part of the survey collection, as they are bound to reinforce that, and to this course the contributor will generally agree. This question of the ownership of the prints belonging nominally to a survey society must be remembered. In my own case, the society provides the prints, but the library provides the mounts, labels, and files, and it does not seem likely that they can be separated from the library. If the society from its own funds provides all these things, and the library only the houseroom for the cabinets, it may be well to have an agreement as to their disposal in the event of the extinction of the society. So far as I know, such a case has not arisen, and it would, I think, most likely be settled by allowing them to remain in the library.

CHAPTER VIII

MAPS AND PLANS

THE basis of all topographical study and its principal record is the map. It seems unnecessary to devote more than a few sentences to so obvious a part of our collection. A careful study of a few works on the history and the making of maps, of which Sir Herbert George Fordham's *Studies in Carto-Bibliography*[1] is as good as any, will indicate what maps must be sought, and certain names of cartographers—Cary, Norden, Camden, Speed, for example—should represent to the collector most desirable items. The old road-books and itineraries, and indeed many other volumes, must never be passed, as they may contain maps and plans of routes, and sometimes of towns and buildings.

The value of the map lies obviously in its representation of the successive divisions and occupations of land, the sites of forests that may have passed, buildings no longer extant, and road-development. The changes in name-forms can be traced to some extent as well. Early maps, made from incomplete surveys, and copies carelessly made, are often inaccurate and cause trouble. It is when several maps are placed in a chronological series and examined that they are

[1] Oxford University Press, 1914.

shown to amplify and to some extent to correct each other. They have many practical uses to-day.

Maps must be treated with much care. Often when received they have been folded badly, are worn at the folds, and are dirty. They can sometimes be cleaned by the methods recommended for cleaning prints, but great care must be taken to preserve the printed surface as the erasure of a single place-name must injure a map seriously. Frail maps may be mounted on a tough paper, but preferably upon muslin, silk, or linen, although this is more expensive. Maps which are likely to be handled, usually tear at the edges, and it has been found practicable to mount such maps on linen and then to fold thin tape over the edges, and to sew this on the map with an ordinary sewing machine.

The accepted method of cataloguing maps is that employed by H. A. Sharp in his *Historical Catalogue of Surrey Maps*, and is as follows:

(1) Enter all maps under the name of the cartographer when known. When it is not, enter under engraver, or publisher, or title—in that order of preference.

(2) Give the scale, in inches, as this is the method common to English maps.

(3) Give the size, first vertically and then horizontally, in inches, to the nearest quarter-inch below actual measurements, of the engraved surface only.

(4) Give the date as printed. An undated map excerpted from another book takes the date of the book. Date others approximately. Historical maps of modern make take the date of the time represented. Reprints should be indicated as such.

94   LIBRARY LOCAL COLLECTIONS

(5) Maps contained in atlases or other works are catalogued individually, but particulars of the author and title of the containing work are given.

It is usual to *arrange* maps chronologically, as this is the most useful method of bringing out the relationships we have shown to be desirable.

An entry of two will indicate the rules.

1610

SPEEDE, JOHN.

Surrey: described and divided into hundreds. Engr. by Jodocus Hondius. 1 in. to 2½ m. 14½ in. × 19½ in. 1610.

1673?

AUBREY, JOHN (?)

Map of the County of Surrey. [No scale.] 9¼ in. × 14½ in. [1673?]. *In* DUCAREL, *Dr*. Some Account of the Town, Church, and Archiepiscopal Palace of Croydon in the County of Surrey: from its foundation to the year 1783.

Plans of towns are treated in the same manner as maps. Plans of buildings and estates should be catalogued under their designer when known, but otherwise the treatment is the same.

MEDALS, TOKENS, AND BADGES

The only argument that the librarian can advance for the collecting of these obviously "museum" objects is that there is no museum in his area to do it for him—they are quite interesting local items. In some towns medals have been struck to commemorate special occasions, as the incorporation of a borough, some special royal visit, the opening of a notable building, and so on; but the method is rare to-day.

Tokens were a method adopted in certain times to supply a kind of local money when small change from the Royal Mint was scarce. Traders in certain towns issued tokens, which were copper, bronze, or even silver coins, usually round in shape, but sometimes of spade or other forms, and these could be used to purchase goods in the town, the issuer of them guaranteeing their value. Boyne's *Trade Tokens issued in the Seventeenth Century in England, Wales, and Ireland*[1] gives the fullest account of these interesting products of local coinage history. Another form of token is that issued as an earnest of payment to be made later for some service rendered. In the early days of fire-fighting the townsmen turned out to help the fire-brigade to extinguish fires, and those who did were paid one shilling, for which they had to apply to the fire-station. Many would apply whose only relation to the fires was that of onlookers, and so tokens were given, on the spot, to those actually doing some work! It was formerly customary to give post office telegraph boys a token for every telegram they delivered, which represented the sum of one penny, the extremely ill pay for which these youngsters once served the public!

[1] Edited by G. C. Williamson. 2 vols. Elliot Stock. 1889-91.

Badges are those worn for special offices or purposes, from that of the Mayor to the member of a local games club. The *seals* of institutions, companies, and societies which are defunct, or have replaced old seals by newer ones, are other items of a "museum" character which may be preserved.

Tokens, badges, and seals should be catalogued under the trader or body by whom they were issued, with cross-reference from the place where they were valid, or generally worn.

[Courtesy of the Chief Librarian and Curator

THE SUSSEX ROOM IN THE WORTHING CENTRAL PUBLIC LIBRARY

CHAPTER IX

THE HOUSING AND FILING OF THE COLLECTION

IN a growing number of towns so great an emphasis is placed upon the collection that it is given a separate apartment. We have already instanced the Edinburgh and Manchester rooms in the public libraries of these cities, and the great towns, almost without exception, have such local rooms. We also instanced the Sussex Room at Worthing as an example of what some smaller places have been able to do. Such provision is most desirable if it is obtainable, and given the opportunity, every librarian will try to obtain it; but he should not wait for such fulfilment. Local material must be collected, recorded, and conserved in advance of that. But where the room is available, a few things have to be considered. Its position, arrangement, and furnishing depend upon whether it is a workshop library, or merely a storehouse. It must, of course, be a storehouse in any case, but if it is to be a workshop, it must be staffed intelligently at all times when the building is open to the public. Alternatively, as might be the case in a small town where readers are relatively few, all shelves, cupboards, and other receptacles must be glazed, or have grills over them, and so may be locked, or otherwise made secure. In some places the local collection room is *en suite* with the reference library, and is always under the supervision of its staff; and in a small town this is possibly the most economical way. But, in any case, free access cannot be given, except in special circumstances and to known workers, to the material in a local collection. Losses from general open-shelf libraries are a necessary, and not altogether negligible, part of their working expenses, and the librarian allows for them, but losses from the local collection may be irreparable, and should not be risked.

No standards have been devised that are generally applicable to the furnishing and arrangement of the room. These suggestions are merely the results of experience and observation, and may, I hope, lead to better ones.

Ventilation, moderate heat, and freedom from the all-pervading enemy, dust, are essentials. These, however, are required for every library for all parts of its stock, and are mentioned here only to place a little greater emphasis upon them for the local collection. If it is possible, the place will be one that is reasonably immune from danger of fire. Charles Johnson has said admirably[1] that where heating is by hot water or steam it should be from a furnace outside the building, and that the wiring for electricity, used either for heat or light, should be carried in iron pipes, and he advocates for the building itself the solidity of concrete

[1] Charles Johnson, *The Care of Documents*, 1919, S.P.C.K.

roof and floors "in view of the development of aircraft attack in modern war." No building of the ordinary sort would survive a direct hit to-day, but such a structure would be safeguarded against an indirect one, or against blast. Where these conditions cannot be met, the librarian provides what substitutes he can, but a collection should be provided with as many safeguards as possible. Every library should have a fireproof strong room of some sort, to hold such records as are irreplaceable. When this cannot be had, a safe at least should be obtained for the most precious things.

The order of the room must be such that every type of material is brought into relation, and in as convenient a way as possible for staff and readers. The readers will not be so many as will be found in any general reference room, but most of them require accommodation for longer periods. The tables should be of a size to permit fairly large books, prints, and the smaller maps to rest on them firmly when spread out; chairs should be as comfortable as modern library practice requires. Much of the furniture will be conditioned by the form of the material and the use to be made of it. The general question of the shelving and housing of the material must therefore be considered.

For books, ordinary shelving, steel or other, will serve. Steel may resist fire better than wood, but it would get red-hot and incinerate its contents in the event of a serious fire. The shelves should be adjustable, and a number of sufficient depth (back to front) for large volumes should be provided. Elephant folio volumes and larger ones would be shelved flat, and shelves which hold only one volume and permit of it being drawn out and replaced easily are made by various library furnishers. Large maps, received on rollers, can be rolled and inserted into cylinders of cardboard which are sometimes covered with cloth. Maps received without rollers may well be provided with them, as this keeps them rigid and ensures correct rolling. The cylinders are filed in various ways, but a case which will hold them vertically as umbrellas in their stand has been found to be as economical as any. This method should be reserved for very large maps. Smaller but still large maps and plans, and posters, cartoons, and similar items can be filed flat in shallow drawers in the plan-cabinets, which are a feature of every architect's office. These cabinets have a desk surface above them on which consultations may be made.

Most of the material is in much smaller form than this. Pamphlets, cuttings, etc., are sometimes filed in boxes, resembling books in shape, and like them, these are placed upon shelves. Occasionally pamphlets are bound into numbered volumes so that they may be shelved and their contents are found by means of index references, but the method means that subjects cannot be kept together in logical order. All pamphlet

HOUSING AND FILING THE COLLECTION 101

boxes and volumes so used are appropriately lettered on the back.

When all methods are considered, there is much to be said for the vertical file for everything in the collection except books and the larger material. The ordinary steel vertical cabinet of foolscap size can be used to accommodate prints, pamphlets, bills, small deeds, maps, clippings, and I have even seen it used for negatives and lantern slides. Experience shows that a folder for each item is the best method in the end, except for a collection of leaflets or cuttings on one topic, and even these should not be allowed to bulk a folder too much. Many of the things can be folded carefully to go into the folders, although there is objection to folding a few kinds of document. It is sometimes urged against deeds, for example, but as deeds almost always are folded when we receive them, and have survived the process for generations, there is not much force in it. It is best to place deeds in envelopes instead of folders, but of the same size, and this additional protection may be given to other things of special value, prints, drawings, and engravings, which might suffer from friction. In the vertical file as already recommended, there should be stout wooden or other dividers at frequent intervals to prevent any sagging of the material.

The files will be arranged in one straight order, classified or otherwise. The result will be a great mobile encyclopaedia of nearly all the important material except books in the collection, into which anything can be inserted, and from which anything can be withdrawn with the minimum of delay and difficulty.

Special materials such as tokens and coins and medals are kept in very shallow drawers divided into small compartments lined with baize or velvet to prevent friction; another method is to place them in small envelopes and to file these vertically in trays or drawers with narrow compartments. Lantern slide cabinets, in which slides file in the same manner as cards in a card cabinet, are standard articles which can be purchased. Similar cabinets can be obtained (or can easily be made specially) for negatives. Although many of the films that a library is likely to acquire are of the non-flammable variety, common-sense requires that every type of film be stored in airtight closed metal cases. They will not as a rule be shelved in any public room, but should be kept, if possible, in a fire-proof room. The outer rim of the container must bear a label with all relevant particulars of the film inside. Such cylinders stand upright upon shelves which have a beading or bar in front to prevent them rolling off. On the general question of films, see Chapter III.

Our local collection room, or that part of the library where the collection is, will thus have to provide many types of accommodation, and much consideration should be given to its probable development so that all the sequences may be maintained with the least amount of displacement. I have as yet been unable to find any method that concentrates the stock more completely than the vertical file, or is more effective if worked efficiently.

Our room must have equipment for readers, and some rules must be observed in its use. Map-measurer, reading glass, T-square, compass, dividers, and perhaps pencils and erasers, should be available. Use of ink should be allowed only under special supervision, and the habit, all too common, of writing on paper placed *upon* the book from which notes are being taken should be politely discouraged. Tracing from maps or prints should again be carefully supervised. A sheet of xylonite or talc should be interposed between the tracing paper and the page that is bring traced. It is well, too, to keep the more popular maps in transparent cases, in which they can be consulted without being fingered. One other word. A place for the reader's hat, umbrella, etc., will induce him not to place them upon the tables or desks. I have even seen a reader, quite unconscious of offence, hang a soaking umbrella on a shelf and allow it to drip over several lower shelves!

Visits should be paid to special local rooms by anyone who contemplates organizing one; we librarians pride ourselves upon our readiness to help each other.

CHAPTER X

MISCELLANEOUS. LIBRARIES OF MUNI-
CIPAL REFERENCE MATERIAL. COPIES.
EXPLOITING THE COLLECTION.
NOTABLE CATALOGUES. CONCLUSION

WE have a few threads to gather together before we dismiss this too brief study of one of the attractive sides of the work of the librarian. Perhaps enough has not been made of this work from the point of view of the librarian in a town which has not much visible romance in its record, or which is so new that its record seems yet to be made.[1] Of these I can only urge that the right attitude is one in which what is happening now, before our eyes, is valued in relation to the future. There is no place that is without a history, even if it is only that of the land itself; its geology is there, its agricultural or other uses, and its present conversion into a dwelling place is surely important. The most drab place has been the scene of many phases of the human drama, and it is no unworthy sentiment which urges the librarian to collect the things that are about him or are near, arrange them, let his purpose be known, and to believe in the future of his task.

[1] But see a valuable article by G. E. Roebuck, "The Collection and Preservation of Local Records in New Areas," *Library Assoc. Record*, v. 38, pp. 546–51, 1936.

LIBRARIES OF MUNICIPAL REFERENCE MATERIAL

These have been established in America, and occasional attempts to provide them have been made here. Funds have not been forthcoming yet for any extensive British experiment in the matter, partly, I suppose, owing to our failure to convince local authorities of the value of a library which contains material of all kinds bearing upon, and published by, local government bodies. It is mentioned here, because its first purpose is to provide an orderly array of the books, reports, and documents—graphic and otherwise—on our area for the use of councils and their officials; its second being to provide supporting material from other areas; and its final purpose being to provide a complete library, adequately administered, of local administration and its records. It would require a suitable room, possibly in the municipal building, access and service at reasonable hours for all who may benefit by it, and it should be the source of all information required by them. It should issue lists of new material on local government, and lists on subjects which become of moment to the Council. It is still an idea to be followed in a propitious time.

COPIES

Where access to original documents is not to be had, copies serve. In fact, as I have suggested already, there are a few documents of such rarity and value that only those readers who have very definite research needs should have direct access to them; for all ordinary purposes copies are as good, especially if they are accurate. Such accuracy is given by the photostat; this is a process which makes a negative of the original on a sensitized paper, from which any number of copies can be printed. It is too expensive an apparatus for any but the large library, but the cost of the individual sheet of copy is about tenpence for a quarto sheet, so that it is within the reach of most libraries. The larger libraries possessing them have shown a willingness to copy at practically cost price, but there are also copying firms which do the work professionally. By the use of the photostat we can sometimes get copies of rare manuscripts which are in private ownership, and for most purposes they are as good as the originals. For the copying of documents of not more than about 12 × 12 inches there is a rapid and exact facsimile photographic copier called the Rotophot which costs under £30. It is useful for the reader who desires to possess a copy of map, broadside, a deed, or even of a print.

Modern librarians are much interested in the rapid development and possibilities of the micro-film. By its use a whole newspaper can be photographed page by page on to what is virtually a cinema film, and this film is now considered to have as much permanence as any well-made paper of to-day. It can, of course, be applied to every form of book or document. A reading apparatus which projects the film so that it can be read easily is a necessary part of the process. There are various makes of micro-films, and the study of them is specially of value to the local collection. The best recent papers on this subject are to be read in the *Transactions of the Federation International de Documentation* at its Oxford Conference in 1938.[1]

EXPLOITING THE COLLECTION

The exploiting of our collection so that it has the maximum of publicity and gives as much service as is possible, is a matter to which much thought could be given, and upon which much could be written. In Chapter III have been discussed the various approaches to holders of things we desire to collect; in addition, we wish to reach the general public, as well as to show those who have placed material in our care that it is valued and used. The exhibition of prints, rare manuscripts, specially-interesting books, and other items, should never cease, and care should be taken to keep our exhibits fresh, and to issue with them explanatory notes and brief catalogues.

Often we can arrange exhibitions of our material at other places in the area. This should be done with

[1] International Federation for Documentation (I.F.D.), XIVth Conference, Oxford–London, 1938. *Transactions*, 2 vols., and vol. of Illustrations and Tables. The Hague, Willem Witsenplein, 6.

discrimination and under most carefully considered safeguards. When prints are exhibited, drawing-pins and other "perforating" methods of fastening them up should not be allowed.

Articles are often welcomed by the local newspapers on subjects covered by the collection, and sometimes accounts of special items. The Press, too, is often quite aware of the value to itself of the collection, and should be encouraged to draw upon it on every possible occasion. In some libraries there are members of the staff who can give lectures on local subjects to societies and churches, as well as in the library itself. This has been my happy experience, members of my own staff have gained for themselves in their own time a real reputation as exponents of local history. Local societies have a warm welcome for them always. It is the same in many other places.

NOTABLE CATALOGUES

A word may be said upon the great catalogues of local literature which must be the pride of the libraries which put them forth. The *Catalogue of the Birmingham Collection*, 1918, with its *Supplement*, 1918–31, which records the collection in the Birmingham Reference Library, is the largest, and together the two volumes contain 2,045 quarto pages, and catalogue about 40,000 items. The finest county catalogue is Roland Austin's *Catalogue of the Gloucestershire Collection*,

1928, a fine quarto, of 1,236 pages, admirably classified and indexed, of the collection in the Gloucester Public Library. It has in it a classification scheme well worth study, and an attractive introduction. *Bristol Bibliography*, which again is of the collection in the Reference Library, 1916, is the title of a portly volume, compiled by the late E. R. Norris Matthews, on "the alphabetico-classed method." A handsome, scholarly work is the *Local Catalogue of Material concerning Newcastle and Northumberland*, issued in 1932 by the Newcastle-on-Tyne Public Library. It is an author catalogue, followed by a classified one. On a small scale, but still a considerable work, is the *Catalogue of the Local Collection* of the Aberdeen Public Library, 1914, which is in dictionary form. An examination of these catalogues is recommended as offering many suggestions as to the material that is collected, and the many ramifications which it may take.

CONCLUSION

All my life I have had before my eyes the picture of the man bending over the open-air bookstall peering for treasures new and old. He lives in an El Dorado closed to the man who is not a book-lover in the sense that all books, wherever they are, possess a magnetic something which compels him at least to find out what they are. He can scarcely bear to leave a good book, of which he already has copies, exposed in the open at an insultingly low price. A true librarian has much of this spirit in him, but he is also, by the terms of his contract with life, a business man, and must direct his enthusiasms. Let him take them towards "local history material," and it will give a purpose to every walk through his own town, and interest to "junk" shops, market stalls, and other weird places. In the end, let him keep his head, and while he determines to have the best local collection in the world, let him remember that system, economy, and discrimination alone lead to success, and that the local collection is but one part of the whole duty of a librarian.

APPENDIX

USEFUL BOOKS AND ARTICLES

THE list is not inclusive. It is a selection of titles of the most useful writings on a much-written subject.

HOW TO WRITE THE HISTORY OF A PARISH
THE LOCAL COLLECTION OF LITERATURE

BROWN, J. D. Local Collections. *In* Manual of Library Economy. Ed. 5, by W. C. Berwick Sayers. 1937. Grafton.

CARNEGIE ENDOWMENT FOR INTERNATIONAL PEACE. Local War Records Committee. Memorandum of Suggestions for Local Organisations with regard to the Preservation and Classification of Local War Records. 1922.

Social and Economic History of the World War: local war records: report of the Secretary to the Local War Records Committee on the year's work, September to September 1920-1: reprinted from History, January 1922.

Includes a classification and schedules of local war records.

COX, J. C. How to Write the History of a Parish: an outline guide to topographical records, manuscripts, and books. 1895.

CRUMP, C. G. History and Historical Research. 1928.

DOUBLEDAY, W. E. Local Collections. *In* A Manual of Library Routine. 1933. George Allen & Unwin.

GROSS, CHARLES. Sources and Literature of English History. Ed. 2, 1915.

HEARNSHAW, F. J. C. Municipal Records. (Helps for Students of History.) 1918. S.P.C.K.

MEADS, D. M. Searching Local Records. *In* R. Engl. Stud., 1928: pp. 173–90, 301–22.

OGLE, J. J. The Free Library: its history and present condition. 1897. Allen.

Local history and literature, pp. 93, 98, 129, 138, 140, etc.

PHILLIMORE, W. P. W. The Parish Historian: a short initial guide for writing, printing, and illustrating the history of a parish. 1905. Phillimore.

In the author's *Parish Registers* is a useful bibliography of parish registers and their history.

Parish Registers: with suggestions for their transcription. 1907. Phillimore.

Other useful works of Phillimore are his *How to Write the History of a Family*, and his *Pedigree Work*, 1914.

THOMPSON, A. H. Libraries and the Study of Local History. *In* L.A. Record, 1927, n.s. v. 5: pp. 1–11.

CLASSIFICATION AND CATALOGUING

AUSTIN, R. The Printed Catalogue of a Local Collection. *In* The Library, ser. 3, v. 8, 1917.

GUILDHALL LIBRARY. Classification of London literature based upon the collection in the Guildhall Library. 1926.

JAST, L. S. *In* Gower, H. D., Jast, L. S., and Topley, W. W. The Camera as Historian. 1916. Sampson Low.

ORMEROD, JAMES. Classification and Cataloguing of Local Collections. *In* Library World, v. 29: pp. 147–51, 168–74, 1926–7.

Pamphlets and Minor Library Material: clippings, broadsides, prints, pictures, music, bookplates, maps. *In* A.L.A. Manual of Library Economy, ch. xxv. 1917.

PHILIP, A. J. Outlines of a Suggested Scheme for the Classification of Local Literature and Antiquities. *In* The Librarian, v. 21: pp. 143, 173, 201, 246, 264, 289, 316, 362.

This series led to outline schemes for various counties in the same journal; i.e. Lancashire, by J. D. Cowley, p. 187; Northampton, by Raymond Irwin, p. 320; and Shropshire, by P. E. Adams, pp. 262, 273.

SAYERS, W. C. BERWICK. Local Collection. *In* Manual of Classification for Librarians and Bibliographers: pp. 277–82. 1926. Grafton.

United States. Library of Congress. Notes on the Cataloguing, Care and Classification of Maps and Atlases: including a list of publications compiled in the Division of Maps and Charts. By P. L. Phillips. 1915.

See the catalogues of the Local Collections of the Gloucester and the Newcastle-on-Tyne Public Libraries for schemes applied.

FILING SYSTEMS

ASHLEY, R. E. A Systematic Scrap-book: loose-leaf binders for clippings, etc. *In* Machinery. 1910. v. 17, pp. 205–7.

BROWN, J. D. Filing and Indexing. *In* Manual of Library Economy. Ed. 5, by W. C. Berwick Sayers. 1937. Grafton.

BURGOYNE, F. J. P. Display and Filing of Periodicals. *In* L.A. Record, 1905, v. 4, pp. 197, 203.

CARABIN, M. A. Detroit Edison Company's Library and its Filing System. *In* Spec. Lib., v. 7, pp. 133–40. 1916.

COLEGROVE, M. E. Material of Current Value: its collection and care. *In* Lib. J., v. 44, pp. 295–8. 1919.
    Vertical files.

DANA, J. C. Filing Pamphlets by the Colorband Method. *In* Lib. J., v. 43, pp. 747–8. 1918.

DOUBLEDAY, W. E. Vertical Files. *In* Manual of Library Routine. 1933. Allen and Unwin.

DRURY, F. K. W. Labor-savers in Library Service. *In* Lib. J., v. 35, pp. 543. 1910.
    Vertical files.

Filing Pamphlet Material. *In* Am. Lib. Annual, 1917–18, pp. 44–5.

Filing and Filing Equipment. *In* Am. Lib. Annual, 1915–16, pp. 48–9.

FITZGERALD, J. E. A Government System of Filing Commercial Information. *In* Spec. Lib., 1917, v. 8, pp. 115–17.

IRELAND, N. O. The Pamphlet File: in school, college, and public libraries. Boston, U.S.A., Faxon, 1937.

KELSEY, J. W. An Up-to-the-minute Geographical Filing System. *In* Lib. J., 1917, v. 43, p. 850.

KERR, E. The Magazine Index and Clipping File. *In* Spec. Lib., 1918, v. 9, pp. 136–7.

MCVETY, M. A., and COLEGROVE, M. E. The Vertical File. 42 pp. 1915. Woodstock, Vermont: Elm Tree Press.

Magazine Binders and Pamphlet Boxes. *In* Lib. J., 1917, v. 42, pp. 436–9.

MARION, G. E. Information Files of Los Angeles Chamber of Commerce. *In* Spec. Lib., 1928, pp. 75–8.

PHILIP, A. J. Filing and Preserving Stock and Records. 2 v. Gravesend: Philip.

Vertical File for Pamphlets and Miscellany. *In* Wilson Bull., 1919, pp. 350–3.

WALLACE, L. E. Filing in the Metropolitan Museum of Art. *In* Lib. J., 1919, v. 44, p. 335.

WARREN, I. Filing and Indexing. *In* Spec. Lib., 1919, v. 10, p. 8.

WINDSOR, P. L. A New Vertical File for Maps. *In* Lib. J., 1910, v. 35, p. 509.

ARCHIVES, DEEDS, MANUSCRIPTS

British Records Association. Report of the Council and List of Members, 1933—*to date*.
   The list of institutional members may be regarded as an address list of the principal archives of the country.

CHRISTOPHER, H. G. T. Palaeography and Archives: a manual for the librarian, archivist, and student. 1938. Grafton.

CLARK, A. C. The Descent of Manuscripts. 1918. Clarendon Press: Milford.

FEARNLEY, A. L. Guide to the Inspection of Deeds. 1933. Pitman.

FOWLER, G. H. The Care of County Muniments. 1923. County Councils' Association.

GALBRAITH, V. H. An Introduction to the Use of Public Records. 1934. Clarendon Press.
   Contains good bibliographies.

GRANT, J. The Preservation of Records. *In* Discovery, 1936, pp. 156–8.

HALL, HUBERT. Studies in English Official Historical Documents. 1908. Camb. Univ. Press.

HALL, H. A Repertory of British Archives. 1920. Royal Historical Soc.

HEADICAR, B. M. Manual of Library Organisation (L.A. Series). 1935. Allen. Chaps. vii and viii.

HEAL, Sir AMBROSE. The English Writing-Masters and their Copy-books, 1570–1800: a biographical dictionary and a bibliography. With an introduction on the development of handwriting by S. Morison. 1931. Camb. Univ. Press.

HUNT, K. G. Origin and Development of the Printed Alphabet. *In* Lib. Asst., v. 21, pp. 5–11, 30–3, 52–61. 1928.

HYDE, D. W. Jr. Our National Archives: a new field of professional effort. *In* Spec. Lib., 1935, pp, 257–60.

National Archives and Our Libraries. *In* Lib. J., 1936, v. 61, pp. 7–9.

JAMES, M. R. The Wanderings and Homes of Manuscripts. (Helps for students of history.) 1919. S.P.C.K.

JENKINSON, HILARY. The Later Court Hands in England, from the Fifteenth to the Seventeenth Century. With separate vol. of collotype plates. 1927. Camb. Univ. Press.

The Librarian as Archivist. *In* ASLIB 5th Conference number. 1928.

A Manual of Archive Administration. Ed. 2. 1937. London: Lund.

Palaeography and the Practical Study of Court Hand. 1915. Camb. Univ. Press.

JOHNSON, C. The Care of Documents and the Management of Archives. (Helps for students of history.) 1919. S.P.C.K.

JOHNSON, C., and JENKINSON, H. English Court Hand, A.D. 1066–1500. Part I, pp. xiii–xxi.

MARSHALL, R. L. The Historical Criticism of Documents. (Helps for students of history.) 1920. S.P.C.K.

NORTON, R. F. Treatise on Deeds. 1906. Sweet.

SAUNDERS, W. Ancient Handwritings. 1909. Simpkin.
    An introductory manual for intending students of palaeography and diplomatic.

THOMPSON, E. M. An introduction to Greek and Latin Palaeography. 1912. Clarendon Press: Frowde.

THOYTS, E. E. (afterwards E. E. Cope). How to Decipher and Study Old Documents. 1909. Stock.

United States. Library of Congress. Notes on the Care, Cataloguing, Calendaring, and Arranging of Manuscripts. By J. C. Fitzpatrick. 1913.

WRIGHT, A. Court Hand Restored. 1912. Stevens.

In the Year's Work in Librarianship, published annually by the Library Association, a chapter is devoted to current work in archives and in palaeography and manuscripts.

The above list on palaeography and archives is confined to works in English. There is a prolific foreign literature which students who would specialize must follow, the main authors being:

French: Arndt, W., Barone, N., Berger, P., Chassant, A. A. L., Chatelain, E., de Bourmont, A., de Wailly, N., Delisle, L., Deprez, E., Géraud, H., Giry, A., Langlois, E. H., Lemoine, P. C., Prou, M., Reusens, E. H. J., Silvestre, J. B., Toustain, C. F., and Tassin, R. P.

118 LIBRARY LOCAL COLLECTIONS

Dutch: Muller, S., Feith, J. A., and Fruin, R.

German: Bresslau, H., Schubart, W., Wattenbach, W.

Italian, Latin: Bonanni, T., Casanova, E., Chroust, A., Fumagalli, Gatterer, J. C., Kopp, U. F., Lowe, E. A., Lupi, C., Paoli, C., Taddei, P., Westwood, J. O.

PRINTS

FREBAULT, MARCELLE. The Picture Collection; as illustrated by the Newark, N.J., Free Public Library. Ed. 4, 1929. N.Y.: H. W. Wilson Co.

GOSSE, C. W. E. Methods of Producing and Preserving Prints. *In* L.A. Record, 1915, v. 17, pp. 265-94, 332-62.

GUNN, M. J. Print Restoration and Picture Cleaning. 1922. Link House.

PLENDERLEITH, H. J. Conservation of Drawings and Manuscripts. 1937. Oxford Univ. Press.

POORTENAAR, JAN. Technique of Prints and Art Reproduction Processes. 1934. Lane.

PHOTOGRAPHIC SURVEYS.

REGIONAL SURVEYS. MAPS

Photographic Surveys

GOWER, H. D., JAST, L. S., and TOPLEY, W. W. The Camera as Historian: a handbook to photographic record work for those who use a camera and for survey or record societies. 1916. Sampson Low.

WARNER, J. Photographic Surveys in Connection with Public Libraries. *In* L.Asst., 1909, v. 6, p. 244.

Regional Surveys

BRANFORD, V. Man and Nature: relation of the sciences and the Humanities. *In* Social. R., 1929, October, pp. 281–92.

BRYAN, P. W. Technique for Recording Land Utilization in City and Rural Surveys. *In* Geography, 1931, September, pp. 211–15.

CARR-SAUNDERS, A. M. Problems of Regional Survey. *In* Publ. Admin., 1934, January, pp. 47–52. Continued discussion, by Henry A. Mess, *ibid.*, pp. 53–7.

FAGG, C. C. History of the Regional Survey Movement. *In* S. Eastern Naturalist, 1928, v. 33, pp. 71–94.

Regional Surveys and Public Libraries. *In* Lib. Asst., v. 13, 1916, pp. 64–71.

FAGG, C. C., and HUTCHINGS, G. E. An Introduction to Regional Surveying. 1930. Camb. Univ. Press.

FLEURE, H. J. Regional Survey and Welfare. *In* S. Eastern Naturalist, 1929, v. 34, pp. 73–82.

ORMSBY, HILDA. Regional Survey in a Large City. *In* Geography, v. 14, 1927, pp. 40–5.

WILLIAMSON, F. Regional Survey and Museums. (Assembling of material.) *In* Museums J., 1929, March, pp. 282–6.

STEBBINGS, W. P. D. Rural Surveys: change, decay, and rebirth. *In* S. Eastern Naturalist, v. 38, 1933, pp. 87–98.

Air Surveys

HART, C. A. [Articles as follows: *In* J. Inst. Munic. Eng., 1937.]: Photography, the modern aid to Surveying, February 16th, pp. 1133–42; Applications of Photography to Surveying, March 2nd, pp. 1181–95; Principles of Surveying from Vertical Air Photographs, March 16th, pp. 1229–46; Preparation of Plans from Vertical Air Photographs, March 30th, pp. 1305–18; Levelling and Contouring from Air Photographs, April 13, pp. 1357–69; Ground Co-operation in Air Surveys, April 27th, pp. 1429–39; Air Photographs and Air Surveys in Civil and Municipal Engineering, May 11th, pp. 1501–16; Air Survey as an Aid to Economic Development, May 25th, pp. 1593–1607.

HEMMING, H. British Progress in Air Surveying. *In* Discovery, 1927, August, pp. 267–70.

Use of Air Photography for Surveying and Economic Development. *In* Photogr. J., 1934, January, pp. 2–13.

HOLST, L. J. R. Topography from the Air. *In* J. Franklin Inst., 1928, October, pp. 435–70.

SALT, J. S. A. Air Survey. *In* J. R. Aeron. Soc., 1933, March, pp. 209–26; and in R. Engineers J., 1935, March, pp. 40–56.

Maps

CRONE, G. R. Cataloguing and Arrangement of Maps. *In* L.A. Record, 1936, v. 38, pp. 98–104.

RICHARDS, E. M. Storage of Maps. *In* Wilson Bull., 1933, v. 7, pp. 356–7.

APPENDIX

WALTON, M. Suggestions for Making Fuller Use of Local Maps and Plans. *In* L.A. Record, 1937, v. 39, pp. 354–7.

See also Library Literature, 1921–1932 (H. W. Wilson Co.) for many earlier articles on Maps.

LIBRARIES OF MUNICIPAL MATERIAL

BROWN, J. D. Libraries of Municipal Reference. *In* Manual of Library Economy. Ed. 5, by W. C. Berwick Sayers. 1937. Grafton.

KAISER, J. B. Law, Legislative, and Municipal Reference Libraries. 1914.

MOORE, H. K. Municipal Reference Libraries. *In* L.A. Record, 1917, v. 19, pp. 497–502.

Consult Library Literature (H. W. Wilson Co.) for references to American practice.

PHOTOSTAT, PHOTO-COPYING, ETC.

BENDIKSON, L. Place of Photography in the Reproduction and Preservation of Source Material. *In* Lib. J., 1934, v. 59, pp. 548–9.

Some Phototechnical Methods for the Preservation and Restoration of the Contents of Documents. *In* Lib. J., 1935, v. 60, pp. 745–6.

BINKLEY, R. C., and others. Manual of Methods of Reproducing Research Materials, 1936. Michigan, Ann Arbor: Edwards Brothers. $3.50.

Perhaps the best book to its date.

BLUMENTHAL, W. Copying Process for Printed Matter without the Use of Photography. *In* Zentralblatt für Bibliothekwesen, Leipzig. October–November, 1915, pp. 321–6.

BROCK, G. C., and DITCHBURN, R. W. Photography of Ancient Manuscripts. *In* Br. J. Photogr., 1933, v. 15, pp. 753-6.

DAVIS, W. Microphotographic Duplication (on 35 mm. film) in the Service of Science. *In* Science, 1936, pp. 402-4.

FISHER, C. P. The Photostat and the Library. *In* Bull, of Med. Lib. Assn., 1917, pp. 22-5; *and in* Lib. J., v. 43, pp. 455-6.

FOX, L. H. Films for Folios. *In* Lib. J., 1937, v. 62, pp. 361-4.

JEFFREE, E. P. Copying Prints: graininess and loss of quality. *In* Br. J. Photogr., 1937, p. 737.

KITTEL, G. H. Photostat: a bibliography. *In* Lib. J., 1929, pp. 316-17.

Micro-photographic Processes in Documentation. (From the ASLIB Conference.) *In* Br. J. Photogr., 1937, p. 805.

PATTERSON, E. F. Application of Small-scale Photography to Library Purposes. *In* L.A. Record, 1936, v. 38, pp. 347-51.

Photography as an Aid to the Historian. *In* Canad. Hist. R., September 1934, pp. 296-7.

The Photostat. *In* L.A. Record, 1913, v. 15, p. 635.

PRATT, V. E. The Micro-copy Film Situation: a discussion of films for library use. *In* Lib. J. 1936, v. 61, pp. 260-3.

RANEY, M. L. Reading Miniature Photo-copy. *In* Lib. J., 1936, v. 61, pp. 136-8.

RUSH, C. E. Micro-photography Abroad. *In* Lib. J., 1936. v. 61, pp. 948-9.

SAVELLE, M. H. History, Photography, and the Library. *In* Lib. J., 1935, v. 60, pp. 873-7.

SCHELLENBERG, T. R. Library Applications of Microcopying. *In* Lib. J., 1935, v. 60, pp. 289-92.

SEIDELL, A. Photomicrographic Reproduction of Documents (on cine-films). *In* Science, 1934, pp. 184-5.

SKERRETT, R. G. Microscopic Big Books. *In* Sci. Amer., 1936, p. 145.

SWINGLE, W. T., and M. K. Utilisation of Photographic Methods in Library Research Work. *In* A.L.A. Bull., v. 10, pp. 194-9, 422-8.

TATE, V. D. Microphotography for the Special Library. *In* Spec. Lib., 1937, April, pp. 115-18; May-June, pp. 145-9.

For recent discussions see the Transactions of the International Federation for Documentation, XIVth Conference, Oxford-London, 1938. The Hague, Willem Witsenplein 6.

SOCIETIES

The librarian will no doubt familiarize himself with the publications of the following societies, all of which in one way or another have a bearing on local collections:

British Record Society.
Historical Association.
Historical Manuscripts Commission.
Institute of Historical Research.
Royal Commission on the Public Records, 1912-19.
Royal Historical Society.
Society of Antiquaries.

Local societies are obvious sources of information and material.

FACSIMILES

Collections of facsimiles to be studied are issued by the following:

British Museum.
New Palaeographical Society.
Ordnance Survey.
Palaeographical Society.
Pipe Roll Society.
Public Record Office.
Selden Society.

INDEX

ABERDEEN catalogue, 109
Air surveys, books on, 120
Aircraft, precautions against, 99
Archives and the library, 21
  books on, 115
Austin, Roland, *Catalogue*, 108
Authors, local, 29, 42
Autograph letters, filing, 72
Axon, Ernest, 34

BADGES, 94–96
Bibliography, 110–24
Biography, local, 43
Birmingham, 28, 69, 80, 108
Boyne, W., *Tokens*, 95
Bristol Bibliography, 109
British Records Association, 36, 49, 55, 64–72
Business records, 26, 27

CATALOGUING, 48–57
  books on, 112
  deeds, 55, 69
  maps, 93–94
  trade tokens, 96
Catalogues, notable, 108
  trade, 44
Classification, 57–63
  books on, 112
  deeds, 69
  Jast's, 84

Church as local centre, 16
  records, 27, 30, 36, 43
Coins, filing, 102
Collecting, 33–47
Copies and copying, 105
  books on, 121
  deeds, 67, 69
  librarian's, 25
Copyhold Acts, 67
Cost, 31–33
Croydon, 9, 24, 44
  Regional Survey, 90

DEEDS, 39–42, 64–72
  books on, 115
  cataloguing, 49, 55, 69
  classification, 69
Dictionary catalogue, 51
Documentation, Féderation International de, 107

EDINBURGH, 22
Election records, 27
Exhibitions, 78, 107

FACSIMILES, publishers of, 124
Fagg, C. C., 90
Filing—
  autograph letters, 72
  books on, 113
  coins, 102
  deeds, 68

126 LIBRARY LOCAL COLLECTIONS

Filing—*continued*.
  films, 102
  lantern slides, 101
  maps, 100
  negatives, 101
  pamphlets, 100
  plans, 100
  tokens, 102
  water-colours, 75
Films, 47–102
Fire precuations, 98
Fordham, Sir H. G., 92
Furniture, 98–9

GALBRAITH, V. H., 72
Glasgow, 28
Gloucestershire catalogue, 23, 108
Goss, C. W. F., 76
Government records, 27
Graphic records, 73–8

HALL, Hubert, 73
Housing the collection, 97–103

JAST, L. S., 9, 59, 74, 80
  local classification, 53, 59, 84
Jenkinson, Hilary, 72
Johnson, Charles, 72, 98

LANTERN slides—
  cataloguing, 56
  filing, 101
Lectures, 108

Librarian—
  attitude to local collection, 110
  as copyist, 25
  as custodian of municipal records, 39
  as producer of material, 37
  as purchaser, 37
Liverpool, 28
Local authors, 26, 29, 42

MANCHESTER, 22, 28
Manorial rolls, 26, 39, 65–72
Manuscript records, 26, 64–72
  books on, 115
Manuscripts, literary, cataloguing, 72
Maps, 28, 92–94, 100
  books on, 120
Matthews, E. R. Norris, *Bristol Bibliography*, 109
Medals, 94–96
Microfilms, 69, 106
  books on, 121
Mounting photo prints, 83, 84
Municipal material—
  reference libraries of, 105
  books on, 121
Municipal records, 27, 38
Music records, 27

NEGATIVES, filing, 101
Newcastle-on-Tyne catalogue, 109

INDEX

Palaeography, books on, 115
Pamphlets, filing, 100
Parish history—
  books on, 111
  records, 26
  registers, 36
Photo-copying, 38
  books on, 121
Photographic Surveys, 79–88
  books on, 118
Photographs, 28, 45–47, 79–88
Photo-process prints, 77
Photostat, 69, 106
  books on, 121
Place names, 16
Plans, 28, 94
  filing, 100
Prices, 31–33
Printed records, 27, 28
Prints, 28, 45–7, 75–8
  books on, 118
Public Record Office, 20, 67

Readers, equipment for, 103
Regional Surveys, 89–91
  books on, 119
Repairing deeds, 67–8
  maps, 93
  prints, 76–7
Roebuck, G. E., 37
Rolls, Master of the, 39, 65–72
Rotophot, 106

Sales, 41
Seals, 68, 70
Sermons, 30
Sharp, H. A., 10, 93
Sheffield, 22
Shelving, 99
Sillick, C. B. M., 9
Societies—
  local, 46
  publishing, 123
Solicitors, the library and, 40
Sound records, 47
Sports records, 27, 45
Stone, Sir Benjamin, 79
Street names, 17
Subject catalogue, 51–3
Surrey, 9
  classification (Jast), 53
  Photographic Survey, 80–88
Surveys—
  air, books on, 120
  photographic, 80–8; books on, 118
  regional, 89–91; books on, 119
Sussex room, Worthing, 23, 97

Theatre records, 27, 44
Tokens—
  trade, 28, 94–6
  filing, 102
Topley, W. W., 63
Tracing, 103
Trade records, 44

Transcriptions, 69
Trials, records of, 30

VERTICAL file, 72, 75, 101
   books on, 114

WATER-COLOUR drawings,
   filing, 75
Walthamstow, 37
Worthing, Sussex room, 23, 97

For Product Safety Concerns and Information please contact our EU representative GPSR@taylorandfrancis.com
Taylor & Francis Verlag GmbH, Kaufingerstraße 24, 80331 München, Germany

www.ingramcontent.com/pod-product-compliance
Lightning Source LLC
Chambersburg PA
CBHW061845300426
44115CB00013B/2506